OSPREY COMBAT AIRCRAFT • 81

ISRAELI A-4 SKYHAWK UNITS IN COMBAT

SERIES EDITOR: TONY HOLMES
OSPREY COMBAT AIRCRAFT • 81

ISRAELI A-4 SKYHAWK UNITS IN COMBAT

SHLOMO ALONI

OSPREY
PUBLISHING

Front cover
On 12 May 1970, Ezra 'Baban' Dotan, veteran Mirage III pilot and CO of No 109 Sqn, achieved a unique feat for an Israeli Skyhawk pilot when he claimed two Syrian MiG-17s shot down over the mountains of southern Lebanon. A vastly experienced combat pilot who had been in action with the Israeli Defence Force Air Force (IDF/AF) since his conversion onto the Mystere in 1958, Dotan had switched to the Mirage III five years later. Serving with No 117 Sqn, he had claimed two Syrian MiG-21s and an Iraqi Hunter destroyed in 1967 (one of the MiGs and the Hunter had been downed during the Seven Day War).

Like a number of fighter pilots, Dotan was transferred to the light attack community when the A-4 Skyhawk entered service with the IDF/AF in 1968. Indeed, he was made commanding officer of No 109 Sqn, which he duly lead until 1971.

On the morning of 12 May 1970, Dotan's unit was flying strikes in support of IDF Operation *Cauldron 2*, which saw Skyhawk units supporting Israeli soldiers and armour in their efforts to mop up Palestinian Liberation Organisation strongholds in the eastern areas of south Lebanon. This offensive quickly triggered a response from neighbouring Syrian, whose air force scrambled a number of MiG-17 fighter-bombers tasked with attacking IDF assets on the ground.

Flying low over the mountainous terrain that was a feature of this part of Lebanon, Dotan and his wingman Giora Ben-Dov ran into a similar number of MiG-17s. A-4 pilots usually ignored enemy attack aircraft when these encounters occurred, preferring to press on with their briefed mission so as to avoid an engagement between roughly equal platforms. IDF/AF fighters were usually on hand to engage Arab attack aircraft in any case. However, with three kills to his name, and anxious to attain ace status like many of his contemporaries from the Mirage III community, Dotan was certainly not your usual light attack pilot! He quickly changed course and hunted down the Syrian MiG-17s, whose pilots had indeed chosen to avoid engaging the Skyhawks. Dotan despatched his first victim with air-to-ground rockets, and then followed this up with a second MiG destroyed with 30 mm cannon fire. These success made Dotan the only IAF pilot to be credited with air-to-air kills while flying the A-4 Skyhawk.

Ezra Dotan passed away on 16 May 1981 following a short illness. He was just 44 years old (*Cover artwork by Gareth Hector*)

First published in Great Britain in 2009 by Osprey Publishing
Midland House, West Way, Botley, Oxford, OX2 0PH
443 Park Avenue South, New York, NY, 10016, USA
E-mail; info@ospreypublishing.com

© 2009 Osprey Publishing Limited

All rights reserved. Apart from any fair dealing for the purpose of private study, research, criticism or review, as permitted under the Copyright, Design and Patents Act 1988, no part of this publication may be reproduced, stored in a retrieval system, or transmitted in any form or by any means, electronic, electrical, chemical, mechanical, optical, photocopying, recording or otherwise without prior written permission. All enquiries should be addressed to the publisher.

ISBN 13; 978 1 84603 430 5

Edited by Tony Holmes and Peter Mersky
Page design by Tony Truscott
Cover Artwork by Gareth Hector, using an A-4 Skyhawk model supplied by Milviz and a MiG-17 model from Wiek Luijken
Aircraft Profiles by Jim Laurier
Index by Michael Forder

Printed and bound in China thorough Bookbuilders

09 10 11 12 13 14 15   10 9 8 7 6 5 4 3 2 1

FOR A CATALOGUE OF ALL BOOKS PUBLISHED BY OSPREY MILITARY AND AVIATION PLEASE CONTACT:

Osprey Direct, c/o Random House Distribution Center,
400 Hahn Road, Westminster, MD 21157
Email: uscustomerservice@ospreypublishing.com

Osprey Direct, The Book Service Ltd, Distribution Centre,
Colchester Road, Frating Green, Colchester, Essex, CO7 7DW
E-mail: customerservice@ospreypublishing.com

www.ospreypublishing.com

CONTENTS

CHAPTER ONE
LIGHT ATTACK AIRCRAFT 6

CHAPTER TWO
WAR OF ATTRITION 18

CHAPTER THREE
YOM KIPPUR WAR 35

CHAPTER FOUR
SKYHAWK SUPREME 72

CHAPTER FIVE
SKYHAWK SUNSET 85

APPENDICES 92
COLOUR PLATES COMMENTARY 93
INDEX 96

CHAPTER ONE

LIGHT ATTACK AIRCRAFT

French fighters dominated the frontline order of battle of the Israeli Defence Force/Air Force (IDF/AF) during the early 1960s. For example, on 1 April 1963 it fielded 36 Dassault Mirage III interceptors, 31 Dassault Super Mystere fighter-bombers, 22 SNCASO Vautour II bombers, 39 Dassault Mystere IV attack aircraft, 26 Dassault Ouragan trainers and 14 Gloster Meteors assigned to a reserve fighter unit. All IDF/AF attack aircraft, with the exception of the Vautour, were fighters that had been reassigned the air-to-ground mission as newer equipment was introduced into service. All Israeli attack aircraft, including the Vautour, were in need of replacement by the mid-1960s.

The IDF/AF's Air Department Weapon Systems Branch (ADWSB) duly commissioned staff studies covering replacements for both heavy attack and light attack jets. In the former category were the Vautour and Super Mystere, whilst the latter aircraft were the Mystere and Ouragan.

The replacement heavy attack aircraft had to boast two engines and be able to attack a target 800 km away with 3000 kg of bombs after an extended flight at low level. A similar low-level mission profile applied to the single-engined light attack aircraft, which was expected to attack a target 400 km away with up to 1000 kg of bombs.

Heavy attack aircraft candidates were the American F-4 Phantom II, the British Buccaneer and the French Mirage IV and Super Vautour proposals. Preferred options for the light attack aircraft were the American F-5 Freedom Fighter and A-4 Skyhawk and an improved French Super Mystere. Despite the staff study having explored the various aircraft types suitable for the IDF/AF's mission tasking, the ADWSB was fully aware that ultimately the jet chosen had to be French. Since 1955, all IDF/AF fighter purchases had involved French machines, for France was the only supplier willing to sell combat aircraft to Israel.

France dominated aircraft sales to Israel from the mid-1950s until the end of the 1960s. During this period, other Western powers were happy with the fact that France had assumed the position of primary arms

Israeli attack aircraft from the early 1960s come together for a unique flypast during an IDF/AF Day airshow. They are, from left to right, the Gloster Meteor, Dassault Ouragan, Dassault Mystere, Dassault Super Mystere and SNCASO Vautour. The Meteor served as an emergency attack aircraft for reservists until 1964, when it was replaced in this role by the Fouga Magister armed trainer. The Ouragan, Mystere, Super Mystere and Vautour were the subject of the IDF/AF's light and heavy attack aircraft replacement studies that eventually resulted in the purchase of the vastly superior A-4 Skyhawk and F-4 Phantom II

supplier to the IDF. However, dependence upon a single source worried Israeli leaders, and the overall quality of the hardware supplied concerned IAF planners. At the time, French combat aircraft were considered inferior to contemporary American and Soviet designs.

The USSR had started delivering advanced weaponry to Arab nations in the Middle East from 1955. Along with the weapons came training, doctrine and advisors. Before too long, Soviet influence had spread throughout the region, threatening moderate Arab nations. Nearly a decade later, the US government realised that it could only observe its stated policy of avoiding advanced offensive weapons export to the Middle East by losing influence among moderate Arab nations. Forced to combat the growing Soviet domination in the region, US policy dramatically changed due to Cold War considerations, and this in turn opened a 'window of opportunity' for Israel.

The decision by the US government to deliver advanced arms to both Jordan and Saudi Arabia triggered the process. The Jordanian purchase of Soviet MiG-21s was considered a realistic option unless a comparable US alternative could be found. The Americans duly offered the the F-104 Starfighter to the Royal Jordanian Air Force (RJAF), and asked Israel not to oppose the sale. The Israelis were willing to agree only if the US government would approve the export of similarly advanced combat aircraft to the IDF/AF.

American and Israeli diplomats gathered in February-March 1965 to issue a vague formula that would allow arms to be traded between the two countries. As a result of this understanding, Israel lifted its objection to the F-104 sale to Jordan in return for a US commitment to supply combat aircraft to the IDF/AF. President Lyndon Johnson's administration stipulated, however, that American aircraft would only be sold to Israel if comparable types were not available for purchase in Europe.

As part of the diplomatic discussions held in early 1965, the Israelis briefly delved into actual IDF/AF operational requirements. It wanted to add a number (75 jets) to the US combat aircraft export commitment. The Americans, in turn, mentioned the B-66 Destroyer as a possible candidate for the heavy attack aircraft operational requirement. However, it was quickly agreed to leave hardware specifics to the military. Israel was asked by the US delegation to prepare a proper request for presentation in Washington, DC.

By then the IDF/AF list of candidates for future combat aircraft had been cut down to the Super Vautour versus the Mirage F2 for the heavy attack aircraft requirement, with the Jaguar as a possible light attack option. A small-scale acquisition of Mirage IVs was also proposed to fulfill the reconnaissance mission. France was keen to preserve its position as sole supplier of combat aircraft to Israel, but the drawback with the French option was that none of the aforementioned heavy and light attack types was expected to be available before 1970. Comparable US combat aircraft were already operational.

Prior to giving its presentation in Washington, DC, the IDF/AF listed American candidates that it had identified as suitable for the heavy and light attack aircraft requirements – the 'offered' B-66 was considered unsuitable and rejected. Instead, the F-4 Phantom II, A-6 Intruder and A-7 Corsair II were evaluated for the heavy attack requirement, while the

A-4, F-5 and F-100 Super Sabre were considered for the light attack role. The resulting IDF/AF procurement programme, christened Plan *Samuel*, called for the immediate acquisition of 30 heavy 120 light attack aircraft. It also recommended the purchase of relatively cheap and simple aircraft that were already in service. Cheap would allow the Israelis to buy a substantial number of jets, and simple would facilitate the swift transition of aircrew from French fighters to American aircraft.

Another Plan *Samuel* guideline emphasised short take-off and landing. The IDF/AF was focused on achieving regional air superiority through its proven technique of systematically targeting enemy air bases. Naturally, IDF/AF planners were concerned about reciprocal enemy attacks on Israeli air bases, and for this reason short take-off and landing (STOL) performance was considered essential when it came to purchasing a new generation of combat aircraft. These concerns in turn led to a preference for US Navy types, which the Israelis considered better suited to STOL.

IDF/AF Commander Ezer Weizman presented Plan *Samuel* in Washington, DC, in October 1965. He stated that the F-4 was the preferred heavy attack aircraft, with the A-6 being an acceptable option, and that the A-4 was the IDF/AF's choice for the light attack aircraft requirement. The immediate American reaction was negative, as it was felt that Israel had requested too many aircraft. The US government also stated that the European acquisition option had not been fully exhausted.

For a while, the Israeli government believed that the opportunity to purchase US combat aircraft was gone. However, behind closed doors, diplomacy forged ahead to the point where, in early 1966, the Johnson administration felt that it was able to comply with the 1965 US commitment to Israel in respect to the supply of arms. In February 1966 US government officials finally presented their 'best offer' to Israel – only 48 examples of the least capable type requested. The Israelis did not try to contest the deal, as they realised that they were being presented with a golden opportunity to introduce two squadrons of urgently needed Douglas A-4 Skyhawks into IDF/AF service.

The draft contract covering the Israeli acquisition of the A-4F Skyhawk was signed in Washington, DC, on 18 March 1966. The deal, which was shrouded in secrecy, was codenamed Operation *Rugby*. With only a handful of government officials in Israel and the US 'in the know' about this purchase agreement, the Johnson administration's announcement in April 1966 that it was approving arms sales to Jordan (which included the F-104) and Saudi Arabia triggered a wave of protests in both Israel and the US. Notification referring to the sale of a 'limited number of tactical aircraft' to Israel followed on 20 May 1966.

Further detailed discussions subsequently defined the configuration of the Israeli Skyhawks. The Americans wanted to downgrade the offensive capabilities of the Operation *Rugby* aircraft, so certain items were made unavailable to the IDF/AF. These included loft-bombing computer logic,

Yossi Sarig (left) shares his Skyhawk experience with IDF Chief of the General Staff Branch Ezer Weizman (centre) during a post-Six Day War visit to Douglas' Palmdale, California, plant. Ezer Weizman was IAF Commander from 1958 until 1966 and IDF Chief of the General Staff Branch from 1966 until 1969. He was widely recognized as the 'father' of the Israeli Skyhawk purchase, having headed up the presentation of Plan *Samuel* in Washington, DC, in October 1965. He was subsequently asked by the Israeli government to revisit the US capital and appeal to the Johnson administration to lift its suspension of Skyhawk deliveries to Israel following the Six Day War. Weizman's mission proved to be a success, for the ban was lifted in October 1967. Ezer Weizman later became the seventh president of Israel in 1993, and served a second term from 1998 through to 2000

AGM-45 Shrike anti-radiation missile launch capability and the rear-radar warning system. Skyhawk-compatible weapons banned from export to Israel included napalm, Rockeye cluster bomb units and the AGM-12 Bullpup air-to-surface missile.

The Israelis themselves waived the AIM-9 Sidewinder air-to-air missile self-protection option, and instead requested the replacement of the jet's TACAN (TACtical Air Navigation) system with a second transceiver. They also opted for a braking parachute, in addition to the arrestor hook already fitted as standard to the jet thanks to its naval heritage. The Israelis also wanted to install 30 mm DEFA cannon in their jets in place of the 20 mm Colt Mk 12s fitted in US Navy A-4s – this modification would not take place until 1969, however.

The end product following all these deletions and modifications was the new A-4H variant, tailored specifically to satisfy American demands for a downgraded Skyhawk, as well as Israeli requirements. The latter requested that the jets be ferried by air directly to the Middle East upon their completion, but they had to agree to shipment by sea instead. Delivery dates were also imposed by the Americans, who stipulated that one aircraft would be handed over per month from September 1967 through to April 1968, followed by four to six aircraft per month from May to December 1968. The $70,160,742 contract for the A-4s was signed on 2 June 1966.

Israel's very first A-4H Skyhawk serves as a backdrop for this photograph, taken at Palmdale in early 1967. Standing second from left is Aharon Yoeli, IDF/AF Attaché in Washington until July 1967, and to his left is his replacement, Uri Yarom

CREW CONVERSION

Operation *Rugby* allowed the IDF/AF to activate a pair of Skyhawk squadrons, and two basing options for these units were explored. In order to simplify the logistical support for the aircraft, the Israelis initially believed that operating both units side-by-side from a single base was preferable. And with IDF/AF engineering experts and logistics officers expecting the jet's service introduction to be difficult due to the Skyhawk being the first American jet combat aircraft to fly in Israeli service, a single location for all aircraft seemed to be obvious choice.

However, the operational plan was to split the Skyhawk force between two bases. If one airfield was neutralised by an enemy air strike, therefore, at least half of the IDF/AF's most modern attack force would still be operational. Basing two squadrons at two bases – one in the south and one in the north – would also improve force flexibility. Operational requirements prevailed. The Skyhawk squadrons were to be split between Ramat David air base in the north and Hatzor air base in the south.

Half of the A-4s would be used to re-equip a Mystere unit at Ramat David, with the rest assigned to a new squadron forming at Hatzor.

The first group of would-be A-4 engineers left Israel for America in December 1966, with the second following three months later. Pilots were scheduled to join the technical staff undergoing Skyhawk conversion in the US from May 1967, again in two groups. The lead group included the two future A-4 squadron commanders, while the follow-up group included the two senior deputy squadron commanders. All four pilots in these senior positions were vastly experienced.

The Ramat David-based unit (No 109 Sqn) was to be led by Ohad Shadmi, who had graduated with Flying School Class 17 in May 1955 and gone on to fly the Mystere during the 1956 Suez War. CO of No 109 Sqn since April 1964, he was to oversee the unit's transition from Mysteres to Skyhawks. Shadmi's counterpart at Hatzor was Yossi Sarig, who had graduated with Flying School Class 19 in January 1956 and flown Meteors during the Suez War. He later commanded Vautour-equipped No 110 Sqn for a year from July 1964, before becoming head of the Operations Branch Attack Planning Section in late 1965. As Sarig recalls, he was then given the task of activating a new Skyhawk squadron at Hatzor;

'IDF/AF Commander Ezer Weizman invited me to join him during the 1965 Paris Airshow. There, we went to the Dassault chalet for a presentation on the Jaguar. Our operational requirement was for an attack aircraft that would be capable of flying a low-low mission profile from Ramat David to the Suez Canal Zone with a certain number of bombs. While examining the presented graphs, I came to the conclusion that the Jaguar was unable to fly this baseline mission profile. I reported my finding to Ezer. He asked me if I was sure, and I immediately replied in the affirmative. He stood up, abruptly ended the presentation and ordered me to follow him out.

'We exited the Dassault chalet in a big fuss and went to the Douglas chalet. Ezer presented himself and asked for the company's Skyhawk presentation. The Douglas response was "We are not ready now, but we will organise a presentation for you this evening at the Hotel George V". That evening three of us – Ezer, Arie Hillel (the Head of Material Department) and I – attended the briefing. I delved into the graphs and quickly realised that this aircraft was absolutely right for us.

'A year later the Skyhawk became a reality for the IDF/AF. I forwarded my name as a candidate for future assignment to the A-4 introduction team. There were two candidates to command the Ramat David unit – Shadmi and I. Both of us were Ramat David "natives". At the time the IDF/AF was divided into "Air Force North" at Ramat David and "Air Force South" at Hatzor. I never served at the latter base except when undertaking Ouragan and Super Mystere conversion courses.

'When I was told that I was to lead the new Hatzor unit, it was suggested that my deputy should be a Hatzor "Air Force South" pilot. I immediately rejected this proposal, and Aki Artzi was assigned as my deputy. He had also served exclusively at Ramat David as a Vautour pilot. When Artzi was injured in a flying accident prior to the Skyhawks' arrival, Zur Ben-Barak, also from Ramat David, replaced him as my deputy. However, Ben-Barak was killed in an accident whilst on the

Senior Formation Leaders' Course, and IDF/AF HQ told me that I was no longer allowed to pick Ramat David pilots for my unit. Nissim Ashkenazi from Hatzor was duly assigned as my deputy.

'As luck would have it, Nissim then suffered an attack of kidney stones that forced him to have an emergency operation, so Arik Ezuz was assigned as my deputy and we attended all the introductory courses together abroad. Nissim eventually recovered in time to participate in the Skyhawk conversion course in Florida too.

'Shadmi and I were scheduled to leave for the US on 5 June 1967, and my boss, Rafi Harlev, who was Head of Air Department Operations Branch, organised a farewell party for me. During the course of this event we received news that the Egyptian army was marching into Sinai. I figured that under these circumstances we wouldn't depart for America, but Rafi reassured me that nothing would happen. Just in case, I made him promise that we would be called back if the situation worsened.

'We left Israel for Florida, then flew on to California for a visit to the Douglas plant to see the production line and discuss the modifications that were being made to our A-4s. Things in the Middle East were tense, and we called Israel twice a day to see if we were needed. Shortly after arriving in California we were indeed recalled. The IDF/AF Attaché in Washington, DC, Aharon Yoeli, organised a flight for us to New York, where we boarded an empty El Al Boeing 707. We were the only passengers, and the airliner was so light that it set a New York to Tel Aviv record of 8 hours and 40 minutes. Shadmi returned to his unit and I returned to the Operations Branch. Immediately after the Six Day War ended, we headed back to California for our Skyhawk conversion course.'

By the time the pilots returned to the US they had even more combat experience. Ohad Shadmi had flown 17 operational sorties during the June 1967 Six Day War as CO of No 109 Sqn, while the unit's senior deputy commander, Hagai Ronen, had completed 19 missions. Finally, Nissim Ashkenazi flew eight sorties in the Super Mystere.

The Skyhawk engineering conversion team personnel had not been recalled to Israel during the emergency, however, being left in situ at Naval Air Station (NAS) Cecil Field, Florida, undertaking their ground school as planned.

During July 1967 the pilots attended an instrument flying course run by VA-45 at NAS Cecil Field. This unit was one of two fleet replacement squadrons for the Atlantic Fleet's Skyhawk community. Having earned their standard instrument clearance rating on 1 August, the pilots were reassigned to neighbouring VA-44 (the second A-4 training unit) for the Skyhawk conversion course – this squadron was equipped with both single and two-seat A-4s.

The IDF/AF personnel quickly learned that the Skyhawk was a simple aircraft to fly. Conversion consisted of eight flights that covered general handling, aerobatics, formation flying and high/low

The first four Israeli pilots to undertake the Skyhawk conversion course in the America pose for a photo between sorties at NAS Cecil Field, Florida. They are, from left to right, Ohad Shadmi, Yossi Sarig, Hagai Ronen and Nissim Ashkenazi. Upon their return to Israel Shadmi and Sarig became squadron COs, with Ronen and Ashkenazi as their senior deputy commanders. At this time there were two deputy commanders in every IDF/AF fighter squadron, with Deputy A being senior and Deputy B junior

altitude navigation. Tactical training followed, with 15 sorties that included a number of innovations for the Israeli pilots – in-flight refuelling, radar handling, landing with cable arresting gear and a catapult take-off. The latter was performed at Marine Corps Air Station (MCAS) Cherry Point, in North Carolina. The final phase of the Skyhawk conversion course took place at MCAS Yuma, in Arizona, where the pilots completed 28 flights covering various aspects of weapons delivery.

Yossi Sarig had vivid memories of his time spent in America;

'The engineering team resided in rented apartments at Jacksonville, but we moved into the Cecil Field Bachelor Officers' Quarters. The very day we arrived at Cecil Field, we saw two Skyhawks taking off together. The leader, whose jet had suffered a deflating tyre as the A-4s accelerated down the runway, drifted sideways and underneath the wingman as they took off, causing a collision. The wingman ejected safely but the leader was killed. This was our first memory from Cecil Field.

'Weapons training was at Yuma, so we made a long flight from Cecil Field that included a night stop en route. We were offered the choice of where to make that stop so we chose San Francisco. We were then told that San Francisco was not on our route, but we insisted. We landed at NAS Moffet Field, spent a nice evening in San Francisco and then continued to Yuma the next day. Yuma was in the desert, but on the day we arrived it was raining so heavily that the base almost flooded.

'Rain aside, flying at Yuma was an amazing experience. Both US Navy and US Marine Corps squadrons regularly rotated to Yuma for weapons training. The local community and press used to welcome every unit and all their pilots, but our mission was top secret. Nevertheless, on our first evening in town all the neon boards flashed *"WELCOME VA-44, WELCOME PILOT YOSSI SARIG"* and so on!

'Flying would start early in the morning because of the heat. Touching the aircraft with bare hands after 1100 hrs was impossible, it was that hot. Pretty soon we had earned a sound reputation for bombing proficiency. Each mission had its own time window on the range, and you had to leave the area on schedule in order to avoid delaying jets coming in behind you. One day we were a bit slow departing the range, and the ground controller urged us to clear the area as another formation was on its way in. The leader of the approaching formation immediately came on the radio and said "No problem. We have heard that they are "hot shit", and we want to see those guys in action". We completed our attacks and they watched us from above.

'While at Yuma, we got friendly with airmen from a US Marine Corps F-4 squadron. One evening we asked their commander for a ride in one of his Phantom IIs. He was a bit surprised, but accepted the request. Early next morning, at 0300 hrs, we met for briefing, took-off at dawn so that no one would know and flew with them in the back seat of the F-4. All of us were already experienced jet fighters that had flown in jets equipped with afterburning engines, so we "secretly" sampled flying the F-4. As already noted, nothing could be kept secret at Yuma, and two days later the local press reported our Phantom II flight. We were the first Israeli pilots to fly the F-4.

'Overall, the Skyhawk conversion course was an enlightening experience. We were senior pilots with a lot of flying hours and many operational missions to our credit, yet flying in America exposed us to different qualifications, especially in-flight refuelling and long range operations.'

SKYHAWK SUSPENSION

The IDF/AF had lost 30 attack aircraft during the Six Day War, and it was therefore looking forward to the introduction of the Skyhawk to help offset these losses. The attrition suffered during this brief but bloody conflict had adversely affected the IDF/AF's plans for the A-4's introduction to service, so Israel forwarded a request to the US government covering the acquisition of an additional 27 Skyhawks.

Meanwhile, the Johnson administration had suspended arms deliveries to the Middle East as part of its diplomatic efforts to stabilise the region once again. This suspension is often mentioned as having delayed the Skyhawk's arrival in Israel. However, test pilot John Lane had actually made the first A-4H flight at Douglas' Palmdale facility on 27 October 1967, some 72 hours *after* the suspension had been lifted.

The first shipment of four Skyhawks left America on 13 December 1967 and docked at Haifa, in Israel, on the night of 29 December. These jets were then transported to Ramat David, from where Ohad Shadmi completed the first Skyhawk flight in Israeli skies on 1 January 1968. Two weeks later Skyhawk Conversion Course 1 commenced with seven students. Their instructors were Shadmi, Sarig, Ronen and Ashkenazi.

Reserve pilots serving with No 109 Sqn who wanted to transition with their unit from the Mystere to the Skyhawk were asked to sign up for a full year of active service. One such individual affected by this order was Arieh Dagan, who was as reserve pilot with the unit from 1960 until 1981. He recalled;

'The message to the reserve pilots in No 109 Sqn who did not want to convert onto the A-4 was that we were to continue flying the Mystere with another squadron at another base as "guests" until our future was decided. A reserve pilot signing on for a year's service would be immediately converted onto the Skyhawk and then allowed to remain as a reservist as part of the squadron after the year was up.

'I initially hesitated when it came to going back into the IDF/AF full time. Having not flown for two weeks, I then received a phone call from Ohad Shadmi. He told me that the wing commander had approved my participation in the Skyhawk conversion course, and that I should prepare myself for four months of reserve service. The following Sunday I started my training on the Skyhawk.

IDF/AF commander Moti Hod (centre) was photographed in front of the first Israeli A-4H Skyhawk on the flightline at Douglas' Palmdale facility in October 1967. The first 48 jets delivered as part of Operation *Rugby* were assigned US Navy Bureau Numbers 155242 to 155289

'Shortly afterwards, the squadron staged a Mystere farewell flypast. This was actually a ferry flight, as the Mysteres were departing Ramat David for Tel Nof. IDF/AF commander Moti Hod approached me during the subsequent reception at Tel Nof and asked me why I had not signed on for a year of regular service to fly the Skyhawk. I was

CHAPTER ONE

overcome with embarrassment! Ramat David Wing Commander Yaakov Agassi was standing right next to me, and he immediately placed his foot on mine and pressed with all his might. Only then did I realise that Moti was not aware of my participation in the Skyhawk Conversion Course!

'I avoided a direct answer by explaining my point of view on the matter. I told him that I did not believe experienced reserve pilots needed a full year to convert to the Skyhawk, nor could they afford to sign up for a year of regular service that would disrupt their normal course of life. Eventually, I paved the way for all of the squadron's reserve pilots.'

IDF/AF fighter squadrons are unique in the way they combine three different types of aircrew within their serving personnel. At any one time, regulars, emergency postings and reservists can be serving alongside one another in a squadron. When a brand new combat aircraft enters IDF/AF service, the training syllabus that is developed for flight crews is set up to deal with large pilot numbers so that units can attain operational capability with the jet in a quick and cost-effective manner. However, there are usually insufficient numbers of regular fulltime pilots in the system to fill the places in these conversion courses. The IDF/AF has found over the years that the only way to achieve economies of scale when training pilots on a brand new aircraft type is to include regulars, emergency postings and reservists on the course at the same time.

This was indeed the case with the cadre of attack pilots destined to fly the Skyhawk, for IDF/AF Mystere units were manned in the main by reservists. Therefore, the composition of Skyhawk Conversion Course 1 was three regulars, three emergency postings and one reservist (Arieh Dagan), despite the IDF/AF stipulation that only fulltime pilots were to fly the aircraft. Skyhawk Conversion Course 2, which opened in April 1968, included two reservists in its intake of nine pilots. The conversion of reservists to the Skyhawk continued surreptitiously until the IDF/AF waived the one year active service commitment.

Although pilot training had commenced, the delivery of A-4s was slower than had originally been anticipated. Indeed, the vessel carrying the second shipment of four Skyhawks did not dock at Haifa until 11 April 1968. Equipment also trickled in slowly. Lacking Triple External Rack (TER) and Multi External Rack (MER) installations like the A-4s

A-4H Skyhawk BuNo 155244 is unloaded at Haifa port on 29 December 1967. The jets were shipped to Israel in batches of three or four as deck cargo. Ships transporting aircraft for Ramat David-based squadrons docked at Haifa, while vessels loaded with A-4s for units at Hatzor and Tel Nof headed for Ashdod. A special white 'cocoon' covering protected the aircraft from the elements during their long voyage from the US

No 109 Sqn's deputies flying Mysteres in trail with their CO, Ohad Shadmi, in A-4H BuNo 155244 tail number 03 (IDF/AF number 5303) over Ramat David during the Skyhawk's first flight in Israel on 1 January 1968. Shadmi performed flypasts over all major IDF/AF air bases during the course of the day, familiarising serving personnel with the sight of the Skyhawk in flight

Israel Prime Minister Levy Eshkol inaugurates Skyhawk operations in Israel at Haifa on 30 December 1967, with A-4H BuNo 155245 in the background. As this photograph reveals, when the Prime Minister cut the ribbon the new Skyhawks were still wrapped up in their white protective 'cocoons', and these were only removed at Ramat David after the jets had completed their transportation from Haifa by road

Having been issued with his letter of appointment as CO of No 102 Sqn (signed by IDF Chief of Staff Yitzhak Rabin) two days prior to the 30 December 1967 Skyhawk reception at Haifa, Yossi Sarig (right) introduces A-4H BuNo 155246 to IDF Deputy Chief of Staff Haim Bar-Lev (centre). The latter would succeed Yitzhak Rabin as IDF Chief of Staff on 1 January 1968

flown by the US Navy, the first four Skyhawks were cleared to lift just three 500-lb and two 250-lb bombs attached directly to the jet's five hardpoints. Although, this was an improvement over the Mystere, which could only carry two 500-lb bombs, it was still way short of the possible ordnance configurations achievable with TERs and MERs. The latter allowed the diminutive jet to lift up to 20 bombs.

No 109 Sqn's aircrew cadre had grown from four qualified pilots in December 1967 to eleven by April 1968, with an additional nine aviators well on their way to completing the conversion course. The first four Skyhawk pilots (Ohad Shadmi, Yossi Sarig, Hagai Ronen and Nissim Ashkenazi) gave the Skyhawk its operational debut in IDF/AF service on 15 February 1968 when they flew two bombing missions against Palestinian Liberation Organisation (PLO) terrorist camps in neighbouring Jordan in the four available Skyhawks.

Four months later, a shipment of three Skyhawks that docked at Ashdod signalled the subsequent activation of No 102 Sqn at nearby Hatzor. Yossi Sarig's letter of appointment as the unit's first CO was dated 28 December 1967, but unlike No 109 Sqn, which was trading its Mysteres for Skyhawks, No 102 Sqn was a new unit that had to be created from scratch. Sarig recalled;

'When we returned from America in late 1967, Shadmi had a place to return to – his Mystere squadron at Ramat David. I was left to report to Hatzor's Wing Commander, Beni Peled. We knew each other well, and as I sat down in his office, Beni said to me, "Yossi, welcome to Wing 4. You are an experienced pilot, so there is little help that I can offer you. I am about to leave here soon in any case. Outside in the parking lot, your pick-up truck is waiting for you. Your secretary is sitting in the cabin beside the driver's seat with her typewriter on her lap. Drive over to Hatzor Wing Flying Squadron Commander Giora Furman, and he will assign you an office from where you can start building your squadron". And that was how we started No 102 Sqn!

'There was only me, Nissim (Ashkenazi), the Technical Officer and his core team at that point. Nissim was in charge of adapting the Wing Flying Squadron building to our needs. I kept myself busy by helping the Technical Officer and his men prepare for the arrival of our aircraft. We also accepted the first two "American" hardened aircraft

shelters (HASs) that had been prepared for us based on an IDF/AF design.

'I was impatient to get the unit up and running, which meant we bent a few rules in order to achieve operational capability. For example, each time a shipment of Skyhawk parts arrived at the IDF/AF Air Logistics Base, our technical team would transport the complete shipment to Hatzor. There, we would check through the containers to see what had arrived from America, keeping half of the parts and returning the rest to the IDF/AF Air Logistics Base for No 109 Sqn. This way we had all the necessary ground handling equipment on strength by the time our first aircraft arrived.

'When the latter were delivered, all we had to do in order to become operational was peel off the jets' protective cocoon covering and upload ordnance onto the hardpoints. Several hours after the Skyhawks arrived we proudly reported to the IDF/AF staff that we were operational. They could not believe it, so we invited them to come and see for themselves. They duly came to Hatzor, saw our readiness status and readily agreed that we were indeed operational.'

The IDF/AF was heavily involved in anti-terrorist operations at this time as the PLO had established a firm foothold in nearby Jordan, from where attacks against Israel were launched. The Skyhawks took part in all four principal 'air policing' missions that dominated the aerial campaign against the PLO – bombing its infrastructure in Jordan, maintaining a quick-reaction alert to attack terrorist groups as they attempted to cross the Israeli-Jordanian border (codenamed *Cricket*), flying visual reconnaissance missions along the Israeli-Jordanian border (*Crab*) and air reconnaissance in force over Jordan (*Grove*). No 102 Sqn's operational debut came on 4 August 1968, when Palestinian terrorist camps in Jordan were bombed.

As the war on the terrorists gathered pace, the last of the 48 Skyhawks purchased through Project *Rugby* was delivered in late 1968. TERs and MERs finally arrived at this time too, and No 109 Sqn flew the first mission with a jet so configured on 2 December 1968 against Palestinian targets in Jordan. Both squadrons had received almost their full complement of aircraft and pilots by end of the year too.

Nos 102 and 109 Sqns quickly appreciated the 'long legs' of the A-4, whose endurance was roughly twice that of previous IDF/AF attack aircraft. Demonstrating this capability, No 109 Sqn Deputy Commander A Yehuda Koren (who ultimately claimed 10.5 kills in Mirage IIIs during the course of four wars with No 117 Sqn – a unique feat) flew a 3 hour 25 minute communications relay sortie over Egypt on 10 December 1968 in support of a long-range reconnaissance mission. In-flight

This No 102 Sqn jet was bombed up at Hatzor to illustrate just how much ordnance the A-4H could carry when fitted with TERs and MERs. The 20 bombs seen here are as follows – 12 250-lb Mk 81 bombs with Snakeye retarding tail fin kits loaded three per TER on the inner wing pylons, a single 500-lb Mk 82 bomb on each of the outer wing stations and six Mk 82s on the MERs attached to the centre fuselage pylon. The A-4's ability to carry so much ordnance was paramount for the IDF/AF when it came to its selection as the light attack aircraft of choice to replace various French types. Typical Six Day War loads for the latter aircraft were just two 500-lb bombs for the Mystere and Super Mystere, two 500-lb bombs and eight rockets for the Ouragan and eight 150-lb bombs for the Vautour

refuelling promised even better endurance, and testing of this new qualification for IDF/AF pilots also commenced in December 1968. Skyhawk pilots were taught how to buddy refuel from either another A-4 or from a four-engined C-97 Stratofreighter that had been modified into a tanker through the fitment of two Skyhawk buddy refuelling pods under the outer wings.

By then a follow-on order for an additional 42 A-4Hs had been signed with the US government, and no fewer than 46 Skyhawks arrived in Israel during 1969. In anticipation of these on-going deliveries, a third Skyhawk squadron was activated during January 1969 at Tel Nof – the first three jets for No 115 Sqn arrived at Ashdod two months later. By then the post-Six Day War clashes between Egypt and Israel had evolved into a full-scale static war along the Suez Canal, which separated Egypt on the west bank and Israel on the east bank. Sporadic IDF/AF operations over Jordan, Lebanon and Syria also continued apace in parallel with the larger scale conflict in the west.

A-4H BuNo 155244 is seen at Ramat David shortly after it had had its protective coating removed. This aircraft became Skyhawk tail number 05 (IDF/AF number 5305), and it served as a No 109 Sqn jet until after the Yom Kippur War, when it was transferred to the Flying Tiger Squadron

No 115 Sqn's A-4H tail number 61 sits between No 109 Sqn's tail numbers 17 and 130 at Ramat David during a turnaround competition – one of the events staged during No 109 Sqn's 18th birthday celebrations, held on 1 July 1969. Sister unit No 115 Sqn was the IDF/AF's third Skyhawk outfit, being activated at Tel Nof in early 1969 with former Mirage III pilot Eliezer Prigat as CO and Udi Shelach (who had also flown Mirage IIIs) as senior deputy. The first three A-4Hs for No 115 Sqn were unloaded at Ashdod on 20 March 1969, and Prigat made the unit's first flight in tail number 62 on 28 March 1969. The unit was officially activated two days later. No 115 Sqn's build-up included the arrival of six aircraft in three pairs on 29 April, 18 May and 21 June 1969, as well as the assignment of its first four regular pilots on 8 May. Initial operational capability had been achieved by July 1969

CHAPTER TWO

WAR OF ATTRITION

Israel's victory in the Six Day War had been decisive, but this was merely one round in an ongoing conflict in the Middle East. Armed clashes along the country's borders continued, while those between Egypt and Israel developed into the War of Attrition that lasted from 8 March 1969 until 7 August 1970. Essentially a static conflict, both sides used artillery, snipers and small scale special operations to ambush the enemy on its own supposedly safe territory.

During this first phase of the War of Attrition, IDF/AF participation was limited. A-4 squadrons continued to attack Palestinian targets in Jordan, but missions over Egypt were limited to communication relay flights in support of heliborne special operations teams. Egypt exploited the strength of its larger regular armed forces, and Israeli casualties totalled 177 (including 50 dead) between March and June 1969.

Extremely sensitive to combat casualties, Israel worried that Egypt's launch of the War of Attrition was a springboard toward a large-scale offensive that would see its forces invade the east bank of the Suez Canal. With effective Egyptian attacks continuing into July 1969, the Israeli government decided that a massive escalation of the conflict was essential to thwart Egyptian plans for a canal-crossing offensive. It also believed that such a campaign would quickly reduce Israeli casualties.

Codenamed Operation *Boxer*, the offensive commenced on 20 July 1969 with air strikes timed to coincide with the Apollo astronauts' landing on the moon. The Israeli government had carefully chosen this moment to attack, as the world's media would be preoccupied with covering NASA's achievements in space, rather than an escalation in the War of Attrition along the Suez Canal. *Boxer's* primary aim was to deny Egypt a canal-crossing option following their successes in the static phase of the conflict. The IDF/AF was expected to achieve this by establishing air superiority over the Suez Canal, suppressing Egyptian artillery and destroying its military infrastructure west of the Canal.

Boxer was spread over a week to cover the entire length of the Suez Canal. D-Day was 20 July 1969, H-Hour was 1400 hrs and the sector of operations was from Port Said to Kantara, in the northern section of the Canal. No 109 Sqn

A No 109 Sqn flight engineer gives the 'thumb up' to reserve pilot Assaf Ben-Nun as the latter guides A-4H Skyhawk tail number 27 out of its hardened aircraft shelter at Ramat David prior to flying an attack mission over Syria on 24 February 1969. Operation *Battery* saw the IDF/AF attacking PLO targets near Maislun, in Syria, with No 109 Sqn launching three four-ship formations with the call-signs 'Peru', 'Congo' and 'Holland'. Assaf Ben-Nun, who was 'Peru 2', flew as wingman to No 109 Sqn's Deputy B Commander Ohad Shadmi (in Skyhawk tail number 12, call-sign 'Holland 1') and Deputy A Commander Yehuda Koren (a Mirage III ace, in Skyhawk tail number 09, call-sign 'Congo 1'). The heavy Israeli bombardments triggered a scramble of Syrian interceptors, and MiG-17s engaged 'Congo' flight. Shadmi expended 70 cannon rounds when chasing a MiG, but the fixed gunsight in his A-4 was far from ideal for air-to-air gunnery and his rounds missed the Syrian fighter

No 102 Sqn flew from Hatzor air base for exactly a year from June 1968 through to June 1969. The unit was then forced to move base after the IDF/AF decided to locate its first Phantom II squadron here. There was no room at the base at the time, however, so one of the four squadrons at Hatzor had to be transferred to Hatzerim in southern Israel. Adhering to the policy of 'last in, first out', No 102 Sqn was ordered to relocate. Unit CO Yossi Sarig strongly opposed the move, so IDF/AF commander Moti Hod agreed to delay it until immediately after Sarig had completed his tour with No 102 Sqn. Nissim Ashkenazi succeeded Sarig as CO on 16 June 1969, and the very next day a 15-ship arrowhead-shaped flypast was staged to signal No 102 Sqn's departure from Hatzor for Hatzerim. Yossi Sarig flew the lead jet in the flypast, and he is seen here landing his A-4H Skyhawk at Hatzerim

was in the vanguard of the action, being tasked the suppression of enemy air defences (SEAD). Once this had been achieved, the air offensive proper would commence. The unit's target was an SA-2 surface-to-air missile (SAM) battery at Gamil airfield, west of Port Said.

Two Mirage IIIs initially strafed the battery's radar, after which two four-ship formations of A-4s attacked the site. The first flew a low-level profile with Snakeye retarded bombs before performing a normal 'pop-up' attack. Simultaneously, a second No 109 Sqn formation was tasked with suppressing a nearby AAA battery. Arieh Dagan recalled;

'The previous evening (19 July), I had a phone call from the squadron and was asked to report at 0500 hrs. Sensing that something big was up, I experienced a restless night – this was usual for me prior to combat.

'The mission briefing was long and detailed, for it was a large-scale operation. I was assigned as No 3 in a mission to attack a 57 mm AAA battery at Port Fuad. Suppression of this battery was essential to enable another formation to attack an SA-2 battery west of Port Said.

'We departed in radio silence and flew low over northern Sinai. We were loaded with napalm, so there was no need to "pop-up". As we came close to our target area the scenery changed from endless desert dunes to white salt swamps. We changed formation into pairs in line astern and accelerated to our top speed. Looking sideways while flying so low and fast was virtually impossible, so we concentrated on the view ahead of us in order to spot our target as soon as possible. Suddenly, port structures and city buildings appeared on the horizon. Seconds later, our leader saw the target and I positively identified the battery, with a gun barrel sat upright in a firing position and several vehicles parked nearby.

'I released my bombs, but before I had even flown over the battery, rolling to survey the battle damage down below, I sensed that my jet had been hit. However, the control column responded normally and the instruments didn't reveal anything untoward. We flew west over the Suez Canal and then turned back. While turning, my wingman reported that he could see flames emanating from my left wing root. Seconds later my hydraulic warning lights began to flash. I levelled off and headed east in a gentle climb. Despite the damage to my jet, it handled normally and the engine responded as per usual, although the hydraulic pressure gauge read zero. My wingman then told me that the fire was spreading along the left side of the fuselage, at which point the fire warning light came on.

'I now started to consider ejecting. My altitude was okay for a safe ejection, but I was flying over a swamp at the time. Our drill for a jet on fire was to immediately eject, but I imagined scenes of swamps from horror films and decided to wait. A few minutes later my wingman reported that my aircraft was no longer on fire. Only a trail of thin white smoke remained, and even this had disappeared within seconds. I chose to stay with the jet and headed for the nearest airfield at El Arish.

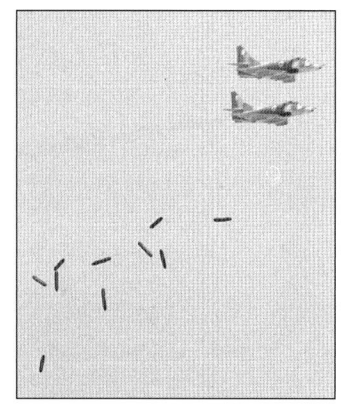

Two Skyhawks demonstrate napalm delivery on 16 July 1970, each jet having released five 'fire bombs'

'En route I climbed, and had my wingman close up to survey the damage. I figured that a hydraulic oil reservoir or tank had been hit, and that the burning fluid was sprayed along the aircraft. The fire was extinguished once all the fluid had been consumed, without causing further damage. To ensure proper communication with El Arish, I activated the emergency generator, by which point I was calm and full of confidence. However, when I extended the landing gear the indicator for the right gear leg did not indicate down-and-locked. My wingman came in close once again and examined my landing gear. He reported that it looked normal. Nevertheless, I decided not to land at El Arish but to fly on to Hatzerim, where proper Skyhawk maintenance was available.

'The failure of the right gear indicator to indicate that it was locked down worried me, so I flew a "touch and go". I then completed another circuit and came in to land. Once on the ground I realised that the brakes were not functioning. It was impossible to remain on the runway without them, and the aircraft drifted to the right, at which point I switched off the engine. The Skyhawk rolled over the gravel beside the runway and eventually came to a stop. I released my harnesses, opened the canopy, jumped down and cleared the area. There was no ambulance, crash tender or firefighting vehicle within sight.

'I waited for a while, and once I was sure that the A-4 would not catch fire, I returned to examine my jet. Damage looked extensive. Many minutes later a vehicle showed up and transported me to the local Skyhawk squadron. From there I pulled rank by taking charge of my wingman's Skyhawk in order to make a swift return to Ramat David.'

Boxer continued until 28 July 1969, by which time the area of operations had been steadily expanded from the northern part of the Suez Canal in *Boxer 1* through to the southern end of the waterway by *Boxer 6*. All three Skyhawk squadrons flew SEAD missions throughout the campaign in support of IDF/AF fighter units that were charged with securing local air superiority over the Suez Canal. A-4 pilots also targeted Egyptian artillery positions and infrastructure.

From the Israeli perspective, *Boxer* achieved its objective of deterring the Egyptians from launching an offensive across the Suez Canal. IDF/AF operations west of the Suez Canal were halted on 28 July 1969, but Egyptian War of Attrition activity continued. Indeed, Israeli troops east of the Suez Canal continued to be targeted by artillery shelling, sniper fire and commando assaults. Despite *Boxer*, the number of clashes climbed from 355 in July to 515 in August. Between March and December 1969, most exchanges on the Suez Canal involved light arms fire (46 percent), artillery (30 percent), mortars (20 percent) and commando assaults (4 per cent).

The artillery fire was particularly troublesome, as the Egyptian army possessed far more heavy-calibre weapons than its Israeli counterpart.

Arieh Dagan's flak-damaged Skyhawk is seen at Hatzerim on 20 July 1969. The No 109 Sqn reserve pilot landed his battle damaged A-4H tail number 26 at the base following an Operation *Boxer* mission. Dagan's wingman escorted his leader to Hatzerim, but as Dagan was a reservist, he returned to his home base at Ramat David in his wingman's Skyhawk while the latter (who was a full-time service pilot) remained at Hatzerim to take care of Skyhawk 26. Luck ran out for this aircraft on 9 September 1969 when it failed to return from a mission over Egypt. Former No 109 Sqn Deputy A commander and subsequent emergency posting pilot Hagai Ronen was reported missing in action

An IDF soldier photographed No 115 Sqn pilot Moshe Melnik carrying out a low-level Snakeye bombing run over Port Inbrahim, in the south sector of the Suez Canal, on 19 August 1969. Seconds later, Melnik's A-4H Skyhawk tail number 62 suffered extensive battle damage. The pilot sensed a minor hit, but he then noticed that the fire-warning light was flickering and the control column was inoperable. Melnik jettisoned the MERs, activated the emergency generator and, using trimming to control his aircraft, pulled up. He headed for Refidim and 'practiced' landing en route, using trim as the only effective control. Melnik convinced himself that he could land safely, but on his final approach the Skyhawk started to shudder violently. Believing that it was too late to eject, Melnik throttled back when the Skyhawk was just ten metres above the runway. Thanks to its rugged structure, the jet remained in one piece despite literally falling onto the tarmac. The left tyre burst, however, causing the Skyhawk to veer off the runway in the direction of fire-fighting vehicles that had been sent out to save the jet. Ignoring the risk of overturning, Melnik managed to steer the Skyhawk away from the rescue vehicles before finally coming to a stop. Transported on a flat-bed trailer back to Tel Nof, Skyhawk 62 was repaired and sent back into action with No 115 Sqn over the Suez Canal in June 1970

Using attack aircraft as 'flying artillery' was the only option available to the Israelis, who were anxious to correct this imbalance. From 13 August 1969, IDF/AF A-4 units flew counter-battery missions as the War of Attrition moved into its next phase. This targeted anti-artillery campaign did little to restrain Egyptian activity along the Suez Canal, however. Indeed, post-war analysis revealed that during this phase of the conflict the shelling actually intensified, despite an increase in IDF/AF missions.

Air superiority over the Suez Canal was essential to ensure that these air strikes could take place without fear of harassment from Egyptian MiG-21s. It was during just such an air superiority operation on 19 August 1969 that the Skyhawk force suffered its first combat loss.

No 102 Sqn had been tasked with attacking an SA-2 battery in the southern sector of the Suez Canal, its pilots planning on performing a low-level delivery of napalm to suppress defending AAA positions. Seconds later another formation of A-4s would also approach the AAA sites at low level and deliver its Snakeyes. With the gun batteries overwhelmed, a third formation of Skyhawks would target the SA-2 site with a conventional 'pop-up' pattern dive-bombing attack. However, during the course of the mission Nissim Ashkenazi (who had succeeded Yossi Sarig as CO of No 102 Sqn on 16 June 1969) was shot down, the A-4 pilot ejecting over the target area into captivity.

A No 115 Sqn Skyhawk was almost lost later that same day when a four-ship formation was tasked with attacking Port Ibrahim, at the southern entrance to the Suez Canal. Loaded with 12 Snakeyes each, the A-4s flew a low-level delivery pattern, during which Moshe Melnik's jet was hit. He managed to land his badly damaged Skyhawk at Refidim, the IAF forward operating base in Sinai. Melnik subsequently became the first F-15 pilot to score a kill in 1979, followed by two more in June 1982. He had previously claimed 5.5 victories flying F-4s.

'TEMPORARY ESCALATION'

Operation *Boxer* had been launched to foil a possible canal-crossing, although with the benefit of hindsight it now seems clear that Egypt was not contemplating such a move in the summer of 1969. And the Egyptian artillery offensive had intensified along the Suez Canal despite the IDF/AF's dedicated counter-battery campaign. Clearly unable to stop the shelling, the Israeli government was keen for a ceasefire with Egypt, but the latter was unwilling to strike such a deal. Anxious to force the Egyptians into accepting a diplomatic solution to the War of Attrition, the Israeli government fully committed the IDF/AF to the conflict in August 1969. The following month, when sortie rates increased, the Israeli government stated that its official policy was 'temporary escalation for the sake of eventual de-escalation'.

The IDF/AF launched its campaign on 9 September 1969, and that same day the Skyhawk community suffered its second combat loss. No 109 Sqn was tasked with supporting a mechanised assault across the Gulf of Suez, and two four-ship formations duly departed Ramat David that morning. The first was tasked with suppressing an SA-2 battery and the second to fly close air support (CAS) for Israeli troops. Although the SAM site was successfully attacked, the CAS Skyhawks (each loaded with six 500-lb bombs and two rocket pods) were forced to loiter over the designated sector waiting to be allocated a target. With the assault proceeding to plan and their patrol time coming to an end, the pilots decided to target a radar station instead. During this attack the four-ship leader Hagai Ronen became separated from the formation. He was last seen hanging beneath the canopy of his parachute over the Gulf of Suez.

This new offensive would see IDF/AF combat aircraft testing the drastically improved Egyptian integrated air defence system. With Israeli air superiority so profound, the Egyptian Air Force (EAF) avoided air combat and chose to improve its SAM and AAA defences instead. This in turn brought the Skyhawk into play, as it had proven to be a capable SEAD platform. However, in October 1969 the IDF/AF's new 'heavy attack aircraft' in the form of the F-4E Phantom II flew its first War of Attrition SEAD mission. Gradually, the latter took over the anti-SAM role from the Skyhawk, although the Douglas jet was still tasked with knocking out AAA batteries, usually in conjunction with F-4s attacking a nearby SAM site. With more Phantom IIs introduced by late 1969, the A-4 was gradually relegated to flying attack missions over the west bank of the Suez Canal, rather than deep into Egypt.

The IDF/AF offensive focused on Egyptian targets on the west bank of the Suez Canal through to the end of 1969, and during this period the A-4 squadrons would routinely launch several missions per day against Egyptian artillery batteries, AAA sites and supporting infrastructure. Nocturnal intruders followed daytime attacks so at to preserve round-

No 102 Sqn A-4H tail number 50 was photographed at Hatzerim on 28 November 1969, having suffered the kind of minor battle damage that did not result in tales of gallantry from the pilot concerned, but was nevertheless a daily reality for Skyhawk units. The IDF/AF end-of-day operations report for 28 November 1969 indicated that Skyhawks, Phantom IIs and Vautours flew 36 attack sorties from 1100 hrs through to 1430 hrs. The reported battle damage assessment from these missions covered strikes on SA-2 batteries, AAA positions, artillery batteries and military infrastructure and fortifications. The Egyptians responded with anti-aircraft fire and at least two SA-7 shoulder-launched missiles. The minor damage inflicted on this particular aircraft was not mentioned in the end-of-day operations report

the-clock pressure on the enemy. Night operations usually involved air reconnaissance in force, with single Skyhawks orbiting over designated 'kill box' sectors and mostly attacking artillery and convoys that revealed their position through firing flashes or vehicle lights. Two-seat TA-4Hs were introduced to the night intruder mission during November 1969.

Running parallel with the offensive against Egypt, Skyhawk squadrons also continued to launch sporadic attacks against PLO targets in Jordan.

With so much combat flying going on, qualified A-4 pilots rarely flew training missions. However, every four months the three light attack units took it in turns to run a Skyhawk Conversion Course so as to infuse the A-4 force with fresh blood. These were mostly new pilots, although there were always a few senior men either converting from older types onto the jet or heading for command positions in the A-4 squadrons.

Although operational activity was intense, it was bearable, as each Skyhawk squadron averaged just four to five combat sorties per day. Therefore, the IDF/AF in general, and the Skyhawk squadrons in particular, could have continued fighting the War of Attrition forever. However, Israel's diplomatic objective *was* a ceasefire.

The offensive, which ran from September to December 1969, is generally considered to have been a success. Air superiority west of the Suez Canal was achieved and Egyptian targets were heavily pounded. But overall fighting along the Suez Canal intensified, the number of Israeli casualties did not decrease significantly and Egyptian will to pursue the War of Attrition remained firm. Still convinced that more military pressure would force Egypt to accept a ceasefire, Israel again escalated the conflict with the commencement of Operation *Blossom* in January 1970. This offensive would see targets bombed all over Egypt, these attacks being made mainly by the new Phantom II force. Skyhawks would fly diversionary strikes and radio relay missions.

Shortly after *Blossom* was launched, the A-4 force suffered its third combat loss. On 16 January No 102 Sqn had been given the task of

Some 25 two-seat TA-4H Skyhawks were procured by the IDF/AF, with the first examples reaching Israel in late 1969. All three Skyhawk squadrons were issued with a handful of airframes each, and they saw combat alongside the single-seat jets thanks to the TA-4H being fully mission capable. In this 25 December 1969 photograph, No 115 Sqn's TA-4H tail number 43 has been laden down with a 'maximum-maximum' bomb load for the benefit of Members of Parliament who were visiting Tel Nof. The jet carries six 500-lb Mk 82s on two MERs under the fuselage, 12 250-lb bombs with Snakeye tail units on two MERs attached to the inner wing stations and six French-era 100 kg bombs on two TERs bolted to the outer wing hardpoints for a total of 24 bombs bombing a section of road just west of the Gulf of Suez. The No 4 jet flown by Dov Peleg did not return – he was listed as killed in action.

Blossom's aim was not to destroy targets in Egypt, but rather to show the leadership in Cairo that the IDF/AF could strike anywhere in the country at will. Israel had clearly signalled that the War of Attrition would not be limited to the Suez Canal in the hope that Egypt's lack of preparedness for larger-scale conflict would drive its leaders to accept a ceasefire. In similar fashion, Operations *Rhodes* was launched on 22 January 1970 as a heliborne assault on Shadwan Island, in the very mouth of the Gulf of Suez. Skyhawk support included the softening up of Egyptian defences through air strikes immediately prior to the helicopter landing of Israeli troops. CAS missions were also then flown.

At this time, No 109 Sqn A-4s debuted as aerial tankers when they completed a dedicated in-flight refuelling patrol for other IDF/AF jets.

The Skyhawk's contribution to the Shadwan operation was significant. Two four-ship formations from No 109 Sqn and one from No 115 Sqn took part in the air strike phase prior to the arrival of the helicopters, and both units flew post-landing CAS missions, which involved pairs of A-4s. During the latter phase of the operation, Ran Goren and Irik Baster from No 109 Sqn and No 115 Sqn's Udi Shelach and Menachem Kashtan intercepted two Egyptian torpedo boats that were spotted heading for Shadwan Island. The No 109 Sqn pair sank one of the vessels with rockets and Kashtan destroyed the other, again with rockets.

This action seriously depleted the fuel levels of the No 115 Sqn jets, and although a No 109 Sqn Skyhawk flying an in-flight refuelling patrol offered them help, the Tel Nof pilots were not yet tanker qualified, so they diverted to the civilian airport at Eilat instead.

Blossom and *Rhodes* did not end the War of Attrition. Instead, the conflict witnessed further escalation when the Soviets intervened following the latter operation. They deployed an entire air defence division to Egypt to bolster the hard-pressed EAF. Once in place, the combined Egyptian-Soviet air defences began to erode IDF/AF gains.

Israel halted *Blossom* in April 1970 in the hope that the Soviet deployment was only aimed at securing Egyptian airspace further west of the Suez. This proved not to be the case, however, for the network of Egyptian-Soviet air defence assets soon began to reclaim territory that had been cleared of these threats by the IDF/AF. The imaginary, but tangible, air-warfare border line that *Blossom* had pushed deep into Egypt gradually moved eastward. The battle for air superiority over the west bank of the Suez Canal that the IDF/AF had won in the autumn of 1969 recommenced in 1970.

Meanwhile, offensive operations against the infrastructure of the PLO spread from Jordan to Syria and Lebanon during this period. Skyhawks attacked targets in Syria from 2 February 1970, and were

Throughout the War of Attrition, the A-4 squadrons ran Skyhawk conversion courses each term so as to feed new pilots into the light attack community. As per IDF/AF tradition, the squadron's groundcrew 'baptised' every pilot after his first solo flight. In this photograph, No 102 Sqn engineers wet down a pilot who has just completed his first solo flight in A-4H Skyhawk tail number 92 on 13 January 1970. That same day, all three Skyhawk squadrons flew missions across the Suez Canal. Nos 109 and 115 Sqns participated in Operation *Blossom 2* while No 102 Sqn undertook 'routine' attack missions west of the Suez Canal tasked to support Operation *Cauldron 2* (an Israeli armoured assault into Lebanon) on 12 May 1970. The objective of the latter offensive was to eradicate the PLO in a sector west of the Lebanese-Syrian border. IDF/AF air strikes of nearby Syrian border posts and artillery positions were planned to safeguard the right flank of the Israeli ground forces.

Skyhawk participation began early on the morning of 12 May when leaflets were dropped over Lebanese towns and villages within the *Cauldron 2* sector. Once the operation was launched, Nos 109 and 115 Sqns were tasked with providing CAS. Armed with rockets, pairs of A-4s orbited over the *Cauldron 2* sector and waited for a call from a forward air controller (FAC). Simultaneously, and high above the Skyhawks, IDF/AF interceptors flew combat air patrols (CAPs), waiting for word from their air-to-air controller to engage enemy aircraft.

Shortly after Ezra Dotan (CO of No 109 Sqn) and his wingman Giora Ben-Dov arrived on station, the latter spotted four unidentified aircraft flying at low altitude. Dotan ordered his wingman to keep the jets in his sight while he tried to determine the identity of these aircraft. Radio calls for identification were not answered, but evoked a response from the IDF/AF fighter controller who reported that the formation was Israeli. He ordered Dotan to focus on his CAS mission. This conflicted with Ben-Dov's next report that he had positively identified four MiG-17s.

Ezra Dotan was a former Mirage III pilot with three aerial kills to his name, so instead of clearing the area and returning to his original mission, he ordered his wingman to lead in pursuit of the MiG-17s. Radio chatter quickly attracted the attention of two Mirage IIIs flying a CAP, whose leader asked Ben-Dov for a vector towards the MiG-17s. Dotan abruptly told them that the MiGs were 'his', and that they should look for other prey! Unperturbed, the fighter pilots dove in search of the MiG-17s, and Mirage III ace Asher Snir eventually claimed one shot down.

The Skyhawks were ahead of the fighters, and they closed on the Syrian jets until Dotan finally saw them and ordered his wingman to open fire. Ben-Dov just missed the trailing MiG-17 with two bursts from his cannon, so Dotan followed up with a rocket attack. He fired 38 projectiles from two of his five pods, but his aim was off and the heavy air-to-ground weapons fell well behind their intended target. The Skyhawk was equipped with a simple air-to-ground gunsight, and this was useless for air-to-air rocket attacks. Having seen his first rockets fall short, Dotan aimed well above the MiG-17 and launched a second salvo from two more pods. This time the projectiles found their mark and the MiG literally vanished within a huge explosion.

Moments later Dotan came under attack from a second MiG-17, its pilot having just opened fire when Ben-Dov told his leader to break away. Dotan threw his jet into a hard left turn, spoiling the Syrian pilot's aim. Just as he was about to complete his turn in order to attack his assailant from the rear, Dotan spotted another MiG-17 flying some 600 metres behind him in a perfect firing position.

The melee continued, with Dotan breaking to the left once again and diving so as to evade this new threat. Yet another MiG-17 overtook the diving Skyhawk, and the Israeli pilot attempted to follow it, but his Skyhawk would not recover from its dive. Realising that he was in trouble, Dotan jettisoned his external stores, including the four empty

CHAPTER TWO

rocket pods. This did the trick, allowing him to recover at very low altitude. Fortuitously, Dotan levelled out right behind the aforementioned MiG-17! He opened fire from a distance of 500 metres but missed.

As so often happens in multi-bogey engagements, the air combat scene suddenly changed from a sprawling dogfight to a two-aircraft duel. The lone Skyhawk in pursuit of a MiG-17 flying very low over mountainous terrain attracted light arms fire from unidentified troops below them. Ben-Dov watched the pursuit from above, keeping an eye out for additional MiGs. Dotan accelerated to 520 knots and closed the distance between him and his target. The MiG-17 pilot, meanwhile, continuously weaved, fully aware of the A-4 right behind him.

Suddenly, the MiG-17 disappeared from Dotan's view. As the latter scanned the landscape ahead of him, the Syrian jet zoomed upwards out of a canyon, still ahead of the Skyhawk but now flying at a much slower speed than the pursuing jet. In haste, Dotan also slowed his A-4 by throttling back its engine and extending its air brakes and flaps. Although he had managed to avoid overtaking the MiG-17, Dotan was now too close to safely open

Smiling groundcrewmen at Ramat David, including the base's Wing Maintenance Squadron commander Norik Harel (centre), greet No 109 Sqn CO Ezra Dotan upon his return from the historic MiG-killing mission over Lebanon on 12 May 1970. Flying A-4H Skyhawk tail number 03, Dotan had successfully engaged Syrian MiG-17s, shooting two of them down. These victories made him an ace (he had claimed three kills whilst flying the Mirage III in 1967), and they were the only air-to-air victories ever credited to Israeli Skyhawks

fire with his cannon. Forced to slow down even more in order to open up the distance between himself and his foe, the Israeli pilot nevertheless stuck with the MiG-17 as it attempted to break away by turning right, reversing to the left and turning right again. This slalom finally placed the Skyhawk in a perfect firing position behind the MiG. Dotan squeezed the trigger and fired a long burst into the jet's right wing root. The wing was quickly ripped away and the jet rolled right and crashed.

Ezra Dotan was flying Skyhawk 5303 during the historic engagement, this aircraft just happening to be the first locally equipped A-4 – fitted with French-designed and Israeli-manufactured 30 mm DEFA cannon. The IDF/AF had used strafing to great effect during the Six Day War, when most of its attack aircraft had been armed with two or four 30 mm cannon. The Israelis, who were accustomed to cannon with a heavy punch, had quickly identified the Skyhawk's internal armament of two Colt Mk 12 20 mm cannon as not being up to the job.

The IDF/AF duly told Douglas that it wanted 30 mm DEFA weapons installed in place of the Colts, and the company designed a structural modification (with the help of Israeli engineers) that allowed them to be fitted. The first examples of the 'upgunned' A-4H were not ready until late 1969, however, when Skyhawks 03 and 34 were handed over to No 109 Sqn. No 22 Air Maintenance Unit at Tel Nof modified those jets already in service, its pilots having flown some 2000 hours during testing of the cannon fit prior to it being cleared for frontline use.

Whether the whole re-gunning effort was worthwhile is questionable, however, for although strafing was important for the Israelis during the Six Day War, it was no longer relevant by the late 1960s. Arab aircraft were now housed inside HASs protected by integrated air defence systems that incorporated both AAA and SAM sites, rather than parked in the open as had been the case in 1967. This in turn meant that A-4 pilots did far less strafing than had been anticipated when the IDF/AF chose to rearm the Skyhawk.

LOST SUPERIORITY

The first signs of an Egyptian-Soviet air defence network 'roll' forward towards the Suez Canal were the construction of numerous trenches in early 1970. These were built in preparation for the deployment of SA-3 SAM batteries. Anxious to delay the latter, the IDF/AF bombed 38 trenches in March, 80 trenches in May and 106 trenches in July. In total, some 310 trenches would be attacked during the War of Attrition.

Night intruder missions were also increased at this time, as the Egyptians routinely exploited the hours of darkness when constructing their air defence network infrastructure.

Despite the best efforts of the IDF/AF, ground-based Egyptian-Soviet air defences were firmly established immediately west of the Suez Canal by late June 1970. All elements were now in place for a direct confrontation between Israeli combat aircraft and Arab missiles.

Five Phantom IIs were subsequently lost in strikes against SAM batteries between 30 June and 3 August. The Skyhawk units were not tasked with attacking these sites at this time, however, pilots sticking to their 'routine' missions against Egyptian artillery and infrastructure targets, as well as performing SEAD.

Assaf Ben-Nun was a reservist with No 109 Sqn (a position he had held since 1960) and an Israel Aircraft Industries test pilot during this period, and he recalled;

'I started flying the Skyhawk when I was an aerospace engineering student. I could have continued flying the Mystere, but I would have had to move to another squadron to do so. I wanted to remain with my unit, so I asked Ohad Shadmi if I could join the Skyhawk Conversion Course ground school. He agreed. When I finished ground school I asked if I could perform a brief check-out in the jet – just six flights – so that the time I had invested in ground school would not be wasted. As I was a reservist, air force HQ's initial response was negative, but I pleaded with them that it was only six flights, and I was eventually given permission. I did my Skyhawk check-out and argued that I would have to fly once a week to preserve my qualification on the jet. After a while my reserve status was forgotten about, and by the end of 1968 I was an operationally qualified Skyhawk pilot.

'The A-4 was a fantastic aircraft, being very reliable, simple to handle and equipped with a zero-zero ejection seat. The cockpit was

Parked beneath camouflaged netting, this aircraft was the 21st Skyhawk delivered to Israel. Given the IDF/AF tail number 34, it was the first A-4 to be rolled off the Douglas production line fitted with 30 mm cannon. Skyhawk 34 was photographed in February 1970 prior to a solo flight event for a new A-4 pilot. Skyhawk 34 subsequently participated in No 109 Sqn's Crystal operational debut in January 1973, although it was lost in action on 7 October that same year

cramped, however, and it was feared that big guys would knock their knees on the edge of the windscreen when ejecting. All taller pilots assigned to fly the Skyhawk were first "tested for fit", therefore. Once they were sat in the cockpit, a crane pulled the ejection seat up and out in order to check whether the pilot could safely egress from the jet.

'Ramat David Wing Commander Yaakov Agassi was the first person to eject from an Israeli Skyhawk. Although he was a big guy, I don't recall him being "tested" to see he he would fit in an A-4. Nevertheless, he ejected safely without injury.

'Another memory I have from this period was the trouble we experienced with the new 30 mm cannon installation in the jet. They were not fitted into the A-4 at the same angle as the 20 mm cannon they were replacing, the DEFA weapons being cocked slightly downwards as in the MiG-17. The thinking here was that a downward angle would allow the cannon to be fired at higher G. However, the results achieved in air-to-air and air-to-ground strafing runs were very poor because the angled weapons were incredibly difficult to aim with the Skyhawk's fixed gunsight. If the aircraft was rolled when diving in order to correct the fall of shot the deflection went sideways. You had to dive in a straight line or else you missed your target.

'The Skyhawk could carry a lot of bombs, but it was equipped with a fixed gunsight. Minimum altitude during attack missions in the War of Attrition was 10,000 ft so as to minimise our exposure to enemy AAA. We were therefore forced to bomb from an altitude of 12,000 ft with that damned fixed sight! Daytime bombing accuracy was, therefore, not high. During nighttime operations we flew lower. We usually operated in pairs during the latter mission, with one aircraft orbiting east of the Suez Canal while the other jet, its lights switched off, crossed into Egyptian territory in search of targets of opportunity. The pilots would switch roles after 15-20 minutes. We bombed and strafed at night from low altitude. Although these nocturnal missions were very demanding, they were also quite successful.'

MiG-21 ATTACK

MiG-21 interceptors were an integral element of a Soviet air defence division. The success of the Egyptian-Soviet air defence network and, in particular, the SAM batteries, encouraged Soviet MiG-21 pilots to be more aggressive. IDF/AF intelligence duly noted the increase in the number of Soviet-flown MiG-21 CAPs and interceptions. Most were not successful, but a close call was recorded during an engagement on 25 July 1970.

Soviet pilots intercepted a pair of No 102 Sqn Skyhawks flying a 'routine' attack mission west of the Suez Canal. The Israeli pilots turned into the MiG-21s, and a brief engagement ensued. IDF/AF fighters on CAP were vectored to the scene, but they were too far away. The Skyhawks disengaged and the dogfight developed into low-level pursuit. A MiG-21 launched an air-to-air missile that homed in on the trailing A-4, and when the jet was engulfed in flames as the weapon exploded, the Soviet pilots broke off their attack and reported an air-to-air kill. The Skyhawk emerged from the conflagration still intact, however, and the damaged aircraft was subsequently put down at Refidim.

Israel's objective of a ceasefire along the Suez Canal front was finally achieved on 7 August 1970 when the War of Attrition officially ended. Soviet intervention had tipped the scales in this regional Cold War era conflict. Israel had been winning the war when the Soviet air-defence division deployed to Egypt in early 1970, and most, if not all, of the of the IDF/AF's hard-won gains in respect to aerial supremacy over the western banks of the Suez Canal had evaporated within a matter of just months. The Phantom II force had failed to destroy Egyptian-Soviet SAM batteries, and suffered losses that forced Israel to accept a ceasefire rather than to compel a ceasefire.

The Israeli Skyhawks' participation in the War of Attrition was extremely successful, however. The jets had flown nearly 6000 operational sorties against targets in Egypt, Jordan, Lebanon and Syria for the loss of just three Skyhawks to enemy action.

At the start of the conflict, the A-4 units performed the whole spectrum of air-to-ground operations, but from late 1969 the Phantom II force took over the long-range deep penetration and anti-SAM missions. This placed a huge burden of responsibility on the relatively small, and new, F-4 force, and many Skyhawk pilots from this period feel that they could have helped out the Phantom II units had IDF/AF HQ given its approval for the light attack squadrons to continue flying these missions. However, the F-4E's inertial navigation system (INS) meant that the jet could attack targets with far greater accuracy than the Skyhawk with its crude fixed gunsight.

The mission division between the Phantom II and the Skyhawk that was implemented during the War of Attrition was adhered to post-war. The F-4 units would attack both long-range and heavily defended high value targets (such as SAM batteries), while the Skyhawks would operate closer to the frontline and provide support (mostly diversion and SEAD) for the Phantom IIs.

The ending of the War of Attrition signalled a period of expansion and strengthening of the Skyhawk force. As a reward for agreeing to the terms of the ceasefire, Israel was given clearance by the US government to acquire additional A-4s, as well as advanced weapons. The latter included AGM-45 Shrike anti-radiation missiles and AGM-62 Walleye television-guided glide bombs. However, the aircraft purchase agreement did not cover the sale of more A-4H Skyhawks as might have been expected. Instead, the *Rugby D* aircraft were surplus A-4Es retired from US Navy service.

Refurbished prior to shipment to Israel, the *Rugby D* jets were actually far better equipped than previous *Rugby* aircraft. The loft-bombing mode had not been eliminated (although this capability had already been added to the A-4H through local modification in Israel) and vital SAM radar-warning receivers were retained. An A-4F style fuselage 'hump' had also been

No 102 Sqn's Skyhawk tail number 24 was initially assigned to No 109 Sqn. Several of the jets flown by Hatzerim-based light attack squadrons had the prefix digit '7' added ahead of the 'tail number' that was actually painted on the nose of all A-4Hs. Skyhawk 24 was photographed during IDF/AF Day celebrations on 16 July 1970 with an impressive weapons display that included 750-lb and 3000-lb bombs in the front row, napalm canisters and 2.75-in rocket pods in the middle row and external fuel tanks and cannon pods in the rear row

Tel Nof-based No 116 Sqn traded its Mysteres for Skyhawks during 1971. The initial *Rugby D* shipment of three A-4Es for No 116 Sqn (IDF/AF numbers 5207, 5208 and 5209) arrived at Ashdod on 18 February 1971. The first A-4E flight in Israel was recorded on 7 March 1971 by the CO of No 116 Sqn in Skyhawk 209. A-4E tail number 11, seen here landing at Tel Nof in July 1972, was the first E-model jet to be locally refitted with 30 mm cannon. The A-4E's DEFA weapons had a downward angle of installation of just one degree following lessons learned from the less than successful 2.5-degree fitment in the H-model Skyhawks

added to the aircraft to house the future installation of an improved weapon delivery and navigation system. Finally, the A-4Es supplied to the IDF/AF had the wiring installed that made them compatible with both the AGM-45 and AGM-62, as well as the AIM-9B Sidewinder air-to-air missile.

Therefore, within a year of the War of Attrition ceasefire coming into effect, the IAF Skyhawk force had almost doubled in size from three to five squadrons. The two new A-4E units were both established outfits converting from French aircraft, No 116 Sqn transitioning from the Mystere and No 110 Sqn from the Vautour. It would have been more 'logical' to convert the former unit to the Skyhawk and the latter to the Phantom II in light of the IDF/AF's original 1960s requirement for both light-attack and heavy-attack aircraft, but the Skyhawk had proven to be so successful in Israeli service that it actually blurred the differences between 'light' and 'heavy'.

Disposition of the Skyhawk force did not change, however, with No 116 Sqn remaining at Tel Nof and No 110 Sqn continuing to fly from Ramat David. The former received its first A-4Es in February 1971 and started its work-ups as a Skyhawk squadron two months later. April also saw No 110 Sqn initiate its conversion with four A-4Hs on loan from neighbouring No 109 Sqn. Both units had achieved operational capability by the summer.

SKYHAWK II

The A-4E acquisition was a quick solution to bridge the gap between deliveries of the two dedicated Israeli Skyhawk models, the A-4H and the A-4N. The latter was based on the A-4M, which was promoted by its manufacturer as the 'Skyhawk II'. A revised canopy profile was the most prominent external feature of the new model. Less noticeable, but no less important, were modified air intakes to feed a significantly more powerful engine. Modified canopy and intakes were common to both the A-4M and A-4N, but the latter was armed with 30 mm cannon and other systems unique to the H-model, including a braking parachute. The A-4N made its first flight in June 1972, and deliveries of the 117 aircraft ordered by Israel commenced in November of that same year.

Prior to this, the IDF/AF had launched a programme to upgrade A-4E/H Skyhawks to A-4N standard in August 1971. Principal

No 110 Sqn at Ramat David was the second unit issued with A-4Es, which replaced its Vautours. The squadron commenced Skyhawk operations in April 1971 with A-4Hs loaned from neighbouring No 109 Sqn pending the arrival of its own *Rugby D* jets. One of No 110 Sqn's first A-4Es was tail number 236, seen here being pushed back into a hangar at Ramat David in July 1971

components of the upgrade were a higher-rated engine and weapon delivery and navigation system. The modified aircraft were dubbed Crystal in IDF/AF service. Each of the major components (higher-rated engine, head-up display and weapon delivery and navigation system) was tested separately in different airframes.

The H-model upgrade received priority over the upgrading of the A-4Es, although all of the latter jets had their cannon replaced. The DEFA installation in these aircraft was slightly different to that in the A-4H, so a prototype installation was initially completed in April 1972. Three months later the 30 mm cannon modification was declared operational, allowing the E-model jets to be upgraded by No 22 Air Maintenance Unit.

The peacetime IDF/AF also sought new roles for the jet within its training command. Purchased as a light-attack aircraft to replace the Ouragan and Mystere, the Skyhawk was also destined to eventually take over the Ouragan's role within the Operational Training Unit (OTU). At that time the IDF/AF year mirrored the Israeli fiscal year (1 April to 31 March), and it was divided into three terms – Term 1 from April to July, Term 2 from August to November and Term 3 from December to March. At the end of each term a Flying School Class graduated, and pilots selected to fly fighters were assigned to the Ouragan OTU during the following term, prior to their postings to frontline attack squadrons. New pilots never went directly to fighter units, as they had to first build up combat experience flying attack types.

No 109 Sqn ran the first experimental Skyhawk OTU course during IAF Year 1970 Term 1 (April to July 1970). The final Ouragan OTU course was completed during IAF year 1972 Term 3 (December 1972 to March 1973). In between these terms, IDF/AF 'top brass' came to realise that the gap between the Fouga Magister trainer that equipped the Flying School Advanced Training Squadron and the Skyhawk was considerably greater than the gap between the Magister and the Ouragan. Therefore, the Flying School Advanced Training Squadron initiated a pilot conversion course from the Fouga to the Skyhawk in October 1972 with the aim of cutting the Ouragan out of the syllabus altogether.

Initially equipped with TA-4H Skyhawks pulled from the three established A-4H units, the Flying School Advanced Training Squadron would soon receive single-seat A-4H Skyhawks too. This was made possible following No 115 Sqn's conversion from the H-model to the A-4N during IAF Year 1972 Term 3. The number of frontline H-model squadrons was now down from three to two, making A-4Hs and TA-4Hs available for the formation of the sixth Skyhawk unit in the form of the dedicated Flying School Advanced Training Squadron. A seventh squadron was also planned for 1973 as A-4N deliveries gained momentum, its primary mission being to serve as an OTU.

CHAPTER TWO

Although the ceasefire between Egypt and Israel was generally maintained from 7 August 1970, clashes along Israel's borders with Jordan, Lebanon and Syria continued. These primarily saw Israeli forces targeting the PLO's terror infrastructure, with A-4s attacking Palestinian targets in both Jordan and Lebanon from 9 August to 4 September 1970. Operations over Jordan wound down from September 1970 when King Hussein launched an offensive against the PLO that eventually saw it expelled from his kingdom. Israel actively supported the Jordanian offensive by sending two-seat Skyhawks across the border to perform visual reconnaissance missions over north Jordan when Syrian armoured forces crossed the border. Hostilities in the country had ended by July 1971, with the bulk of the PLO now being concentrated in Lebanon.

The Skyhawk units then enjoyed a brief break from their 'routine defence' activity until January 1972 due to the PLO having to suspend its operations whilst reorganising in Lebanon. The only combat seen by the A-4 squadrons during this six-month period of inactivity came during Operation *Toaster* on 18 September 1971. A SEAD mission was flown by F-4s that were responding to a rare skirmish over the Egyptian-Israeli ceasefire line, the Phantom IIs launching AGM-45 Shrike anti-radiation missiles against Egyptian SAM batteries whilst two four-ship formations of No 116 Sqn Skyhawks flew diversionary air strikes. Shrike-armed A-4s also flew anti-radiation attack patrols in the wake of the unsuccessful *Toaster* strike, but this flare-up over the Suez Canal subsided. The IAF still had no answer to the challenge posed by the powerful Egyptian air defence force.

On the northern Israeli border, the IDF/AF's anti-terror campaign resumed on 24 January 1972 when Skyhawks attacked a PLO camp in Syria. A sustained campaign of attacking Palestinian targets in Lebanon and Syria followed from 25 February to 9 March 1972. On the last day of this round of air strikes, No 115 Sqn flew a mission in the prototype A-4H Crystal (IDF/AF number 5359), and its pilot reported that the new weapon delivery and navigation system performed flawlessly.

Skyhawks also participated in Operation *Chick*, which saw large-scale air strikes mounted against PLO targets in Lebanon. This evolved into Operation *Crate B* on 21 June 1972. *Crate B* was a special mission that targeted a group of senior Syrian officers undertaking a commanders' tour of the Israeli-Lebanese border. The Syrian officers were taken prisoner to be used as a bargaining chip in negotiations to release Israeli PoWs. *Crate B* achieved its objective and *Chick* motivated the Lebanese government to restrain PLO activity north of the Israeli-Lebanese border.

Although the Lebanese authorities clamped down on Palestinian cross-border activity, they could not stop the PLO from 'exporting' terror overseas. When the Palestinian Black September group attacked the

The IDF/AF's sixth Skyhawk unit was the Flying School Advanced Training Squadron. Formerly equipped with Fouga Magister trainers, the unit was officially activated with Skyhawks on 8 October 1972. Its TA-4Hs had come from all three A-4H squadrons, including tail number (1)45 seen here, which had previously served with No 109 Sqn. Although the TA-4Hs remained fully operational despite their training role, the small cadre of instructors assigned to the Advanced Training Squadron and led by unit CO Ran Goren had their own emergency postings in the event of war. Therefore, the flying school's Skyhawk squadron was not expected to fight as a unit in an emergency, but act instead as an operational reserve that could supply combat-ready aircraft wherever they were needed most

Olympic village in Munich, Germany, on 5 September 1972 and murdered 11 Israeli competitors, the IDF/AF responded with a large-scale anti-terror campaign. Air strikes were symbolically launched on 8 September 1972 against 11 Palestinian targets in Lebanon and Syria.

By then, five of the IDF/AF's ten attack squadrons were equipped with Skyhawks, and they flew the bulk of the air-to-ground sorties during the campaign that followed. The fourth, and final, day of combat operations during the relatively quiet period between the War of Attrition and the Yom Kippur War came on 8 January 1973, when Syrian mortars were targeted.

Although actual combat had been rare for the Skyhawk units from August 1970 through to October 1973, many new attack pilots and been allowed to build up vital operational experience during this time. Improved versions of the jet had also been allowed to bed in, with the A-4H Crystal receiving a valuable shakedown in frontline conditions with No 115 Sqn prior to it being given its combat debut by No 109 Sqn on 8 January 1973.

GOLDEN EAGLE SQUADRON

By the summer of 1973, the Skyhawk was the most numerous combat aircraft in Israeli service. The IDF/AF could field six fully equipped squadrons, one operating the A-4N unit, two the A-4E and three the A-4H. Five squadrons were frontline attack units and the sixth was the Flying School Advanced Training Squadron. And although the latter was not classified as an operational unit, it was flying fully combat-capable aircraft that could be used as a ready reserve in an emergency.

All three Skyhawk models in Israeli service were undergoing some sort of modification and/or certification at this time. The A-4N was a relative newcomer, and this meant that it was still going through the usual in-service process to achieve operational certification of all planned capabilities. The A-4H and A-4E Skyhawks were still being rotated through upgrade programmes that would see the jets fitted with higher-rated engines and an improved weapon delivery and navigation system

The introduction of the A-4N into IDF/AF service was conservatively planned so that the total number of operational Skyhawk squadrons would remain at six throughout the process. No 115 Sqn was the first to embark on the transition from A-4H to A-4N, the unit starting in early 1973 with the arrival of Skyhawk tail number 322. It was to be a gradual swap, however, for the unit was still flying a few A-4Hs in October of that year. In line with IDF/AF practice, No 115 Sqn's A-4N transition had not yet been completed when Tel Nof-based A-4E operator No 116 Sqn started its conversion to N-model jets in the autumn of 1973

CHAPTER TWO

that resulted in them being designated Crystal aircraft. They were also being fitted with 30 mm cannon. The improved self-defence offered by air-to-air missiles that the IDF/AF had originally rejected was now also being added to the A-4E (AIM-9B Sidewinder) and tested on the A-4H (indigenous Rafael Shafrir 2) from late 1972.

In line with continued deliveries of A-4Ns, the IDF/AF planned to convert No 116 Sqn from the E-model to the N. Its now-redundant A-4Es would in turn be issued to a new seventh Skyhawk unit. Christened the Golden Eagle Squadron (it was never numbered), the unit was activated at Etzion air base in Sinai in August 1973 with six former No 116 Sqn jets. After getting itself up to speed operationally, the Golden Eagle Squadron assumed the OTU mission from IAF Year 1973 Term 3. Meanwhile, No 116 Sqn had commenced its transition to the A-4N by loaning four jets from No 115 Sqn.

The latter unit suffered a major blow on 3 October 1973 when its CO, Ami Gadish, was killed in an accident. Tel Nof air base commander Ran Ronen proposed that Giora Rom should fill the leadership void at No 115 Sqn, but IDF/AF Commander Beni Peled said no. Ronen insisted, however, despite the fact that Rom had never previously flown a Skyhawk and had not seen a single day's service with his new unit prior to his acceptance of command at noon on Friday, 5 October 1973. Rom was anything but a novice when it came to combat though, having been the IDF/AF's first ace, and a veteran of several painful months as a PoW in Egypt after being shot down by a MiG-21 in September 1969.

Little did Rom know when he accepted the position that his first Skyhawk flight 24 hours later would see him targeting Egyptian troops attacking an IDF outpost on the northern edge of the Suez Canal!

No 109 Sqn CO Yoram Agmon (also an ace with two kills in the Mirage III and four in the F-4E) flew A-4H Skyhawk tail number 32 when the unit gave the Crystal upgrade its operational debut on 8 January 1973. Agmon and his wingman successfully targeted Syrian mortars that were shelling IDF outposts. The primary identification feature for jets that had had the Crystal upgrade was the avionics 'hump' on top of the fuselage. Not all 'humped' Skyhawks were Crystal-equipped, however, as many of the surplus A-4Es supplied to Israel by the US Navy were handed over with empty dorsal avionics bays

Ten Golden Eagle Squadron A-4Es bask in the sunshine at Etszion air base on the eve of the Yom Kippur War. The seventh IDF/AF Skyhawk unit, the Golden Eagle Squadron was activated on 1 August 1973 with ex-No 116 Sqn aircraft. It had been created in order to perform the OTU role, but the Yom Kippur War erupted on 6 October 1973, disrupting IDF/AF plans

YOM KIPPUR WAR

The Skyhawk was the standard IDF/AF attack aircraft and the most numerous type of fast jet in the Israeli inventory on the eve of the October 1973 Yom Kippur War. Seven squadrons were equipped with the aircraft at four bases across Israel. The status of these units varied from fully operational to non-operational as follows;

No 109 Sqn at Ramat David was fully operational with the A-4H.
No 110 Sqn at Ramat David was fully operational with the A-4E.
No 115 Sqn at Tel Nof was fully operational with the A-4N.
No 116 Sqn at Tel Nof was transitioning from the A-4E to the A-4N.
No 102 Sqn at Hatzerim was fully operational with the A-4H.

Flying School Advanced Training Squadron at Hatzerim was equipped with the TA-4H and A-4H. The unit was not considered operational, as its instructors had their emergency postings and the school's combat-capable jets were an important operational reserve for frontline units.

Golden Eagle Squadron at Etszion had only a handful of A-4Es on strength and was not operational.

Therefore, only five of the seven Skyhawk units would see combat during the Yom Kippur War. Golden Eagle Squadron aircraft were handed over to the two operational A-4E units on 6 October 1973 and No 116 Sqn returned the loaned A-4Ns to No 115 Sqn. The Flying School Advanced Training Squadron instructors were ordered to report to their emergency posting units and Golden Eagle Squadron pilots were temporarily assigned to the two operational E-model units.

IDF/AF planners rated No 115 Sqn as being fully mission capable with its new A-4Ns, which meant that it would fly all manner of attack missions including air base strikes and SEAD. The principal tasking for the A-4E-equipped units was CAS. The A-4H squadrons were barely operational, however, as they had some jets already equipped with the Crystal weapon delivery and navigation system, others still undergoing modification and still more that had yet to be upgraded. This meant that a large number of A-4Hs were rated as unserviceable. Still, there were 160+ jets in the inventory on 6 October 1973, which was enough to support five units of 24 aircraft apiece, and still have operational reserves.

A high state of alert had already been implemented on Friday, 5 October 1973, but an IDF intelligence evaluation ruled out the possibility of a full-scale Egyptian-Syrian attack. This in turn meant that readiness was somewhat relaxed within the IDF/AF, and personnel had been allowed to go home on weekend leave so as to properly observe Yom Kippur on the 6th – the Jewish Day of Atonement.

The first IDF/AF Skyhawk loss of the Yom Kippur War was Squadron 109's A-4H Skyhawk tail number 87, in which reserve pilot Hanan Eitan was killed. Skyhawk 87 (then 187) was photographed at Ramat David in October 1971 during a wing turnaround competition. (via author)

The realisation that large-scale conflict was in fact imminent finally registered with the IDF during the early hours of Saturday, 6 October 1973. All personnel on leave were hurriedly called back to their units, as were emergency postings and reserves.

Israeli plans for war depended heavily on the IDF/AF achieving air superiority within 48 hours. Until then, troops on the ground could expect only limited air support as attack aircraft would be vulnerable to enemy fighters, SAMs and AAA. Once air superiority had been secured, unrestricted air support would ensure Israeli victory. Since conflict was imminent, the IDF/AF was ordered to prepare for a pre-emptive strike that would initiate the two-day air superiority battle. The targets were Syrian SAM and AAA defences. However, at 0700 hrs on the 6th this was changed to Syrian air bases because of unfavourable weather forecasts.

The Israeli government's exact decision-making process after 0700 hrs on the morning of 6 October 1973 still remains unclear some 36 years later. Apparently, it rejected the pre-emptive strike option at around 0920 hrs, but this decision did not properly filter down the chain of command, for at about that time IDF/AF fighter and light attack squadrons were briefing Operation *Goring Syria* – widescale attacks on Syrian Air Force (SyAAF) bases. Among the targets assigned to Skyhawk units were airfields in Damascus (No 110 Sqn), Dmer (No 110 Sqn), Hama (No 109 Sqn), Khulkhul (No 116 Sqn), Nazariya (No 116 Sqn) and Saikal (No 102 Sqn). H-Hour was 1130 hrs, and at 1100 hrs pilots were already in the cockpits of their jets preparing to taxi out and take-off when word finally arrived at the various bases that *Goring Syria* had been cancelled.

The halting of this operation triggered confusion and disbelief among the frontline units that had been preparing for the strike throughout the morning. Convinced that *Goring Syria* would be as successful as the pre-emptive strikes some six years earlier, the personnel at air bases across Israel were now forced to anxiously wait until the Arab nations made their move. At 1400 hrs sirens sounded at every IDF/AF airfield as Egypt and Syria launched simultaneous coordinated attacks. In the north, Syrian forces breached the anti-tank obstacles in the Golan Heights, and in the south Egyptian troops crossed the Suez Canal into Sinai.

The IDF/AF's grand plans for total air superiority over the battlefield were immediately scrubbed and small formations of fighters were scrambled in haste. The first aircraft to take off were vectored toward enemy jets over the Golan Heights and the Sinai Peninsula, although fewer than ten were actually engaged. Skyhawks tasked to fly CAS missions over the front followed the interceptors, with the first four-ship formation departing Ramat David at 1415 hrs.

Scrambled A-4s faced two major obstacles. The IDF/AF's plan of securing air superiority had not happened, so the EAF and SyAAF controlled the skies over their respective frontlines. And with Israeli troops having been caught by surprise, there was no proper system of FAC support in place to facilitate effective CAS operations. The Skyhawk pilots flew into harm's way without knowing what their targets were. A lack of information from the battlefield and no air superiority degraded mission effectiveness and resulted in additional combat losses.

The first Skyhawk formation to take off also suffered the first combat loss of the war. Syrian SA-2 SAMs shot down the lead jet as the division flew over the Golan Heights at medium altitude in search of targets, killing reserve pilot Hanan Eitan. His wingman had to jettison his bombs so as to evade more SAMs, and the trailing pair hastily attacked nearby Syrian border posts that were probably irrelevant to the actual fighting.

The fate that befell this first formation, and the effectiveness of its attack, were representative of Skyhawk actions during Day 1 of the war. From the outbreak of hostilities at 1400 hrs until sunset at 1721 hrs, the A-4s flew in four-ship formations over both fronts. Air strikes did not affect events on the ground, however, and three more jets were lost – one over Syria and two over Egypt. All three pilots ejected.

Among the aircraft to see action that day were four A-4Ns from No 115 Sqn at Tel Nof. Tasked flying a CAS mission over the north sector of the Egyptian front, the formation leader was Yachin Kochva, who had his brand new CO, Giora Rom as a wingman. The latter described the mission in his autobiography, *Tulip 4*;

'I was holding, No 4, for takeoff on runway 33. I was in an A-4N with two external fuel tanks and eight Mk 82 bombs. It was 1500 hrs on Saturday, 6 October 1973. The target was Egyptian forces attacking an IDF outpost on the northern edge of the Suez Canal. Sound normal for a fighter pilot? It seemed so, except that although I was No 4, I was the unit CO, and when I took off it would be on my first flight in a Skyhawk – a jet that I had never flown before. Very few pilots in the history of air warfare had flown a combat mission as their first sortie in a new aircraft.

'Three days earlier, the CO of No 115 Sqn had been killed in an accident. When I got home that night to Hatzor, there was a message from IDF/AF commander Beni Peled. He wanted me to assume command of the unit. I immediately drove to Tel Nof, where No 115 Sqn was based, to see Ran Ronen. "You know that I have never flown a Skyhawk?", I told him. "I want you in this position", he replied. "The squadron is in a state of shock. Do whatever it takes tomorrow and on Friday, and next week you will take an A-4 conversion course".

'Within the first 48 hours of assuming command I attended Ami Gadish's funeral, met squadron personnel and visited Gadish's widow. I then stayed overnight at Tel Nof on Friday because of heightened alerts.

'On Saturday morning at 0700 hrs sirens rang across the base. We were moving to Alert Status 3. Briefings were then held for air base attack missions in Syria, with H-Hour set at 1130 hrs. I was still in my dress uniform at this point, so fellow pilot Rami Yosef drove to my house in Hatzor to bring me my flight suit and boots. Pilot Mickey Schneider, who, as my No 2, would be shot down by a Syrian SA-6 missile five days later to become a prisoner of war, brought me a G-suit and torso harness from wherever they keep this stuff on the squadron.

'The pre-emptive strike was not approved, so I desperately tried to schedule a familiarisation flight in my new aircraft. An A-4 in HAS 10 was stripped of its external loads. Pilot Avraham Yakir accompanied me to the jet and helped me strap in. He explained the layout of the cockpit, the head-up display system, the INS alignment process and how to start the engine. I did it step-by-step and then taxied out to the runway.

'I couldn't close the canopy, however. You had to pull hard – something you never do in the elegant Mirage III, so I was a little too hesitant. Yakir jumped on the wing and helped me close the canopy. I headed for runway 33 and requested permission for takeoff. It was exactly 1400 hrs. The tower replied, "Peach", return to your line – Egyptian aeroplanes are en route to attack the base!" Yakir was waiting for me with a car in the HAS. I was whisked back to the squadron building. Pilots in flying gear were on the balcony with maps and aerial photos. Taking maps and photos from one of them, I asked "Who is your leader?" "Yachin" he answered. Yachin was my first student in the pilot training course. "Yachin, I am your No 4. If I have any questions we'll talk on the red radio". Each aircraft had two UHF radios, red and green.

'After takeoff, it would take 20 minutes to our initial point from where we began our high-speed, low-level run-in toward the pop-up manoeuvre. During this time I would learn to fly the Skyhawk.

'Yachin requested permission for takeoff. I asked him what speeds we used in our configuration. "Lift nose at 125 and takeoff at 150", he replied. We were quickly airborne, heading south. The aeroplane responded to my commands and I tried to position myself comfortably in the cockpit. Yachin helped me with the ammunition switches and explained how to make a dive-toss attack. Once over the initial point we descended in preparation for the attack.

'Reserve pilot Uri Bina was section leader. He called "Three pulls" over the radio and I pulled with him into a pop-up manoeuvre for the first time in my life in a Skyhawk. I rolled onto my back at 6000 ft and dove. The yellow glow of an SA-2 missile came toward me from Port Said, at which point I thought to myself "is the whole world against me today?"

'I tried to execute the attack and rejoin Uri Bina. "Four, your bombs didn't release" Uri called. I returned to the initial point before heading back to the target once again, this time alone. The rest of the flight waited for me. It was now time to fly my second pop-up attack in an A-4. This time, I made a continuous computing impact point (CCIP) run and felt eight bombs drop from the aeroplane toward the amphibious armoured vehicles that I could clearly see between the coast and the outpost.

'Yachin requested a fuel check on the way back. One, Two and Three reported having 4500 lbs each while I looked for the fuel gauge. I finally found it in the lower righthand corner of the front panel. It was showing only 1800 lbs, however. I immediately realised that I had not activated the fuel transfer from the reserve tanks. In the Mirage III, fuel transfer was automatic – no switches had to be moved. I reported 4500 lbs too! I was, after all, the squadron CO, and I didn't want anyone to realise that I was struggling with certain aspects of the jet! Where was the bloody switch for the fuel tanks? When I couldn't find any fuel panel I extended my hand backwards to the left and started systematically turning all the switches in the cockpit to ON. The fuel gauge continued to drop to 1600 lbs, but over El Arish, at 20,000 ft, it began to slowly rise again. I made a note that after landing I would find out which switch did the trick.

'"Four, 150", Yachin called over the radio in the frugal language of aerial communication, and I circled in the jet over Tel Nof, stabilising it at 150 knots for my final approach. I put Skyhawk 417 gently down on runway 33, then taxied back to HAS 10. I was in a rush. I had a squadron to command, I didn't yet know all the pilots and I couldn't remember the Technical Officer's name. I also had only one Skyhawk sortie in my logbook, and there was now a war on.'

All four jets fron No 115 Sqn had returned safely to base on this occasion. That was not to be the case for other units, however. Amongst those downed on 6 October was Yanki Yardeni of No 110 Sqn, who became the first Skyhawk pilot to eject during the Yom Kippur War. He was flying as wingman to the squadron CO in a four-ship formation that had taken off from Ramat David at 1526 hrs in search of targets over the Golan Heights. Yardeni had yet to drop his bombs when a Syrian SA-2 hit his Skyhawk and tore it apart. The pilot ejected from within the inferno, injuring his legs in the process. Yardeni came down amidst the battlefield and ran for cover, ignoring his wounds.

It was already dusk by the time Israeli tanks found Yardeni, but as they were heading east to fight the Syrian army, they could not evacuate either him or a wounded soldier inside another tank. After several hours of combat in the dark, an M3 halftrack evacuated them both to safety.

Next to eject was Yishay Katziri of No 102 Sqn, who departed Hatzerim as 'Pulse 3' at 1630 hrs with orders to attack Egyptian forces in the northern sector of the Suez Canal. He and his three squadronmates had no target intelligence or location, just orders to 'go and get them'. Flying west into the setting sun, the 'Pulse' pilots had just pulled up from low-level in search of targets when an SA-7 hit Katziri's Skyhawk. He ejected, but again suffered leg injuries in the process, as well as fracturing his right hand. Landing in salt swamps east of the Suez Canal, Katziri was found by two Israeli tank crewmen that had survived an Egyptian commando ambush that had disabled their tank. It is possible that the same commandos had also launched the SA-7 that downed the A-4.

The two soldiers attempted to carry the injured pilot, but when this proved impossible one of them left Katziri in order to find help. The remaining tanker and the A-4 pilot hid all day under the canopy of the latter's parachute, but they failed to spot a helicopter that was reportedly sent to their rescue. After sunset on Sunday, 7 October 1973, the second soldier also went in search of help too. Figuring that linking up with friendly forces at night would be dangerous, he waited for morning and then successfully found Israeli troops. They had also met up with the first tanker several hours earlier. Katziri's location was quickly reported to IDF/AF HQ and an elite force was tasked to rescue the pilot.

However, at 0900 hrs on the morning of Monday, 8 October, two Egyptian soldiers found Katziri and took him prisoner. Two hours later the elite force also arrived at the scene, exchanged fire with the Egyptians and had a soldier killed, after which they retreated.

The third Day 1 Skyhawk ejection also involved a pilot from No 102 Sqn. Reservist Mati Karp departed Hatzerim at 1700 hrs as 'Watt 3'. His mission was generally similar to that flown by 'Pulse' flight earlier in the day, except this time Karp was operating over another

Squadron 110's A-4E Skyhawk tail number 235 was lost over the Golan Heights on 6 October 1973. The pilot Yanki Yardeni ejected and was retrieved. A substitute A-4E was later delivered to Israel as part of the US emergency aid and became Skyhawk tail number 835. (via author)

sector, north of Great Bitter Lake. His four-ship formation pulled up in a hail of flak and bombed concentrations of Egyptian troops west of the Suez Canal that were presumably waiting to cross into Israel.

During post-strike evasive manoeuvring something hit Karp's Skyhawk, forcing him to eject. He too suffered the now-customary leg injuries. Everything had happened in such a rush that Karp was unsure as to whether he was flying east or west of the canal at the time of his ejection. Once on the ground, he discovered that his survival radio was inoperable too. Karp decided that he was still west of the canal, so ignoring his injuries, he headed further west so as to avoid the frontline.

As the sights and sounds of war got closer, the A-4 pilot realised that he was actually east of the canal and marching towards the frontline! Turning back, Karp pulled a transistor radio out of his pocket, but was only able to tune into a station that was broadcasting a concerto! Listening to this, the injured pilot hobbled along in the darkness towards a road. He soon spotted several tanks, but unsure as to whether these were Egyptian or Israeli, Karp waited for them to pass before heading off along the road once again. A short while later he noticed a deserted Israeli Military Police tent that was full of rations. Karp satisfied his hunger and renewed his march along the road, still listening to his concerto.

Hearing more tanks, he hid beside the road until he heard the crews speaking Hebrew and then linked up with them. The time was 2300 hrs, six hours after take-off. The tanks had just evacuated injured troops from the frontline and they were waiting for an IDF ambulance. When the latter showed up, the injured pilot was taken to hospital.

Skyhawks continued harassing Egyptian and Syrian forces during the night of 6/7 October, and a fifth Skyhawk was lost at 1830 hrs when a No 102 Sqn jet failed to return from a nocturnal intruder mission over the Suez Canal. The pilot, Ehud Sadan, was killed. Flying a low-altitude loft-bombing attack at night against a wall of SAMs was a hazardous task that was seldom practiced. Many senior pilots who flew these sorties returned with horror stories of near misses during evasive action in the dark against dazzling trails of fire from SAMs.

Around midnight, a maritime battle in the Mediterranean Sea north of Sinai's coastline resulted in an Israeli Navy request for air support. Two F-4Es were scrambled from Tel Nof loaded with bombs and flares – one aircraft would illuminate while the other attacked with its bombs. However, a jet had to abort and the mission spares went unserviceable, so two bombed-up, flare-equipped, A-4Es from No 116 Sqn scrambled to support the lone Phantom II. The jets took it in turns to illuminate and bomb, and they were credited with sinking an Egyptian missile boat.

Preparations for Day 2 operations were made during the night. The air superiority battle would at last commence on the morning of 7 October with the implementation of IDF/AF Master Plan *Challenge 4*. Its primary objective was to destroy Egyptian SAM batteries west of the Suez Canal. The plan was to fly four successive waves. The first would suppress AAA fire along the Suez Canal and neutralise seven Egyptian air bases, while the second, third and fourth would destroy SAM sites in the northern, centre and southern sectors of the Suez Canal, respectively. If *Challenge 4* was successful, the IDF/AF expected to achieve air superiority over the Egyptian front by the end of the day.

During Day 1 of the war, the IDF/AF had not operated in line with pre-war doctrine. The air superiority battle had not been launched and attack aircraft were forced to go up against alerted enemy AAA and SAM sites. Skyhawk pilots were scrambled to fly CAS without essential intelligence. Proper targets were not available, and employed tactics were in contradiction to pre-war training. As a result, A-4s were lost flying at medium altitude over SAM-defended zones or when loft-bombing at night. The chaos, and losses, of Day 1 triggered a crisis in confidence between staff planners and frontline warfighters. This crisis may have been forgotten had Day 2 plans resulted in the securing of air superiority over the Suez Canal. This did not happen, however.

Skyhawk operations on the morning of 7 October were divided between CAS and air superiority. The two A-4E squadrons were tasked with CAS over the Golan Heights and along the Suez Canal, while the three A-4H/N squadrons were assigned to *Challenge 4*. The launching of the latter has been shrouded in controversy ever since.

The IDF/AF could not instigate simultaneous air superiority offensives over two fronts. The Israelis were keen to knock out Egypt ahead of Syria, as it was believed that Egyptian forces were stronger, and therefore posed the greater threat. However, the IDF's evaluation that the Israeli forces' situation in Sinai was worse than in the Golan proved to be wrong on the morning of Day 2. Israeli troops in the Golan were struggling to hold their positions just as much as their comrades in Sinai. And while the latter was a huge buffer zone that protected Israel, Syrian forces invading the southern sector of the Golan Heights posed an immediate threat to Israeli towns and villages. By the time this was realised, *Challenge 4* was already underway. A decision was reached at IDF high command to press ahead with the first wave of attacks, but then discontinue the air superiority battle over the Egyptian front so that the IDF/AF could turn its attention north and launch an air superiority offensive against the SyAAF.

The first wave of *Challenge 4* was actually meaningless when it came to achieving air superiority, and post-war analysts treated it as an anachronism. Egyptian air bases were hardened against air strikes and the EAF was not the IDF/AF's opponent in the air superiority battle over the Suez Canal. Amassing 100+ attack aircraft to raid eight Egyptian air bases had no impact on the air superiority battle over the front.

Likewise, the suppression of AAA sites along the Suez Canal was only effective if immediately followed up by attacks on nearby SAM batteries, which were the principal opponent of the IDF/AF in the air superiority battle over the Suez Canal. Post-war analysis suggested that *Challenge 4* should have targeted the SAM batteries right from the first wave, skipping the first suppression wave and starting with the second destruction wave.

Most *Challenge 4* Skyhawk sorties were flown over the Suez Canal against AAA sites. This was a hazardous mission, and two jets

A-4H Skyhawk tail number 60 was a Squadron 115 aircraft until it was handed over to Flying School Fighter Advanced Training Squadron based at Hatzerim, where this image was taken in 1973. When the war broke out, Skyhawk 60 was handed over to neighbouring Squadron 102 and was lost in combat on the morning of 7 October 1973; pilot Shai Avital was killed. (via author)

CHAPTER THREE

were lost – a No 115 Sqn Skyhawk (flown by reserve pilot Shimon Ash, who was missing in action) and a No 102 Sqn jet (killing reserve pilot Libi Daller). Compared to the AAA hell encountered over the Suez Canal, the deeper-penetration airfield attacks were almost 'milk runs'.

No 109 Sqn was tasked with attacking Shubra Khit to the west of the Nile Delta. Time-over-target was 0725 hrs, and the attacking force included two four-ship formations. All eight No 109 Sqn Skyhawks tasked with flying this mission were A-4H Crystal airframes. The CO of of the unit led the first formation and reserve pilot Arieh Dagan headed up the trailing four-ship. The lead formation was tasked with bombing the runway, while Dagan and his men were to bomb a nearby radar compound. Cloudy skies complicated the strike, but eased disengagement from MiG-21s that attacked the rear A-4 formation. One opened fire at Dagan's No 4, but all the Skyhawks evaded the fighters.

Bombing HASs was of no value to the war effort, and IDF intelligence reported that Shubra Khit was not neutralised, despite damage to its main runway, for operations continued from the secondary parallel runway.

No 115 Sqn was also tasked with attacking an EAF airfield at 0725 hrs, six of its A-4Ns departing Tel Nof to raid Mansura, in the Nile Delta. This mission was a combined operation with F-4Es, which were to target runways while the Skyhawks hit a command post. Again, bombing was not perfect and MiG-21s intercepted the attackers over the target. All the A-4s returned safely to Tel Nof, nevertheless. IDF intelligence reported that operations from Mansura continued unabated.

Only meagre scattered forces remained of the IDF regular divisions on the Golan and Sinai fronts by the morning of 7 October. Reserve divisions were hastily rolling forward to bolster the defences, but the IDF high command had identified a dangerous void in the frontline defences until the arrival of these reserves. The only way to back up the hard-hit regular divisions was with the IDF/AF. CAS missions were immediately launched over both the Golan Heights and the Suez Canal in parallel with the ongoing battle for air superiority.

The two A-4E units were in the forefront of the Day 2 CAS effort, and they both had to operate against intact air defences. They also suffered from a lack of intelligence in respect to the location of enemy forces on the ground. No 110 Sqn's first CAS mission saw a four-ship formation depart Ramat David at 0502 hrs. The pilots orbited over the Mediterranean as they waited to be called in to attack targets, but when they finally ran low on fuel they jettisoned their bombs into the sea and returned to base. Subsequent formations were, however, assigned targets to attack – mostly Syrian armour, which was defended by mobile AAA, shoulder-launched SAMs and a still-intact air defence force network of SAM batteries. No 110 Sqn lost one jet (with reserve pilot Rafi Lev killed) and at least two others suffered battle damage.

The initial CAS split for the Skyhawk force saw Ramat David-

Squadron 109's pilot Giora Bar-Ner departed Ramat David at 0800 on 7 October 1973 as section leader tasked with attacking Syrian armour along the Golan Heights' old IPC road. While approaching target, A-4H Skyhawk tail number 36 was damaged, possibly by anti-aircraft fire since the aircraft did not show the nozzle damage typical of an SA-7 surface-to-air missile hit. Bar-Ner made an emergency landing at Ramat David where the runway's net stopped the aircraft, which was still loaded with bombs. (via author)

A-4E Skyhawk tail number 211 was originally a Squadron 116 aircraft but was handed over to the Golden Eagle Squadron at Etszion where this photo was taken on 19 August 1973. The Skyhawk was no longer adorned with the Squadron 116 badge but did not carry a Golden Eagle Squadron badge because this unit did not have an approved badge yet. Since the Golden Eagle Squadron did not achieve operational status by 6 October 1973, its aircraft and service personnel were on temporary assignment to other Skyhawk squadrons during wartime. Skyhawk 211 was returned to Squadron 116 on 6 October 1973 and was lost the next morning over the Golan Heights. *(via author)*

based No 110 Sqn supporting Command North over the Golan Heights and Tel Nof-based No 116 Sqn supporting Command South over the Suez Canal. This changed at 0700 hrs on Day 2 when No 116 Sqn operations were shifted from south to north too. Just 90 minutes later the unit lost a jet over the Golan Heights. It was one of a pair of A-4s assigned to fly battlefield air interdiction over the Kuneitra-to-Damascus road. The Skyhawk suffered battle damage while making a hazardous low-altitude visual reconnaissance run along the road looking for targets, and the reserve pilot ejected over friendly forces.

The official IDF history of the Yom Kippur War attributes the stopping of the Syrian advance in the southern Golan Heights to CAS. Available IDF/AF data indicates that 56 air strikes were flown from dawn at 0538 hrs until 1000 hrs, 40 of which were over the southern sector of the Golan Heights. The flipping between fronts continued throughout Day 2, for at 0940 hrs IDF/AF commander Beni Peled ordered all available air support, including No 110 Sqn, to Command South. The Golan Heights was duly emptied of CAS assets just two hours before the start of a brief, but violent, battle for air superiority over the Syrian front.

By then the IDF/AF knew that *Challenge 4* had been an abject failure. Only one of the seven EAF bases attacked had possibly been neutralised for any sustained period of time, and the Suez Canal AAA suppression effort had been a pointless waste of time. Obviously, it is possible that *Challenge 4* might have succeeded had all four waves been despatched on Day 2. However, this was not to be, as IDF high command decided that Syria posed a greater threat. The IDF/AF was ordered to shift its air superiority campaign from the Sinai front to the Syrian front. *Challenge 4* was discontinued and units were told to prepare for Operation *Model 5*. Its objective was the suppression and destruction of SAM sites east of the Golan Heights, with time-over-target set at 1130 hrs.

Unlike *Challenge 4*, *Model 5* did not boast a full-scale suppression wave. Instead, loft suppression of Syrian AAA batteries was planned to start at 1120 hrs in direct support of the follow-up main force that was tasked with destroying SAM batteries from 1130 hrs.

No 110 Sqn A-4Es launched AGM-45 anti-radiation missiles, while Nos 109 and 116 Sqns despatched four and five pairs, respectively, to loft-bomb AAA positions. No 115 Sqn's contribution to the main force was five formations tasked with dive-toss bombing SAM batteries, and one of the pilots involved in this vital mission was reservist Itzhak Golan;

'I was a Vautour squadron deputy commander until 1967, when I became a staff officer. I organised a one-day A-4H check out for myself in 1969, with ground school in the morning and two flights in the afternoon. The first was in a TA-4H with an instructor in the back seat and the second was my solo. My emergency posting at the time was as a Mirage III pilot, but I continued to occasionally fly the A-4 so as to preserve my qualification.

'In 1970 I left active duty to fly for El Al, and my emergency posting squadron converted from the Mirage III to the Phantom II. This happened almost simultaneously, and I was presented with two options – assignment to another Mirage III squadron at a different base or switch to the Skyhawk, also with another unit, but at the same base, Tel Nof. I preferred the Skyhawk/same base option, and became an A-4 reserve pilot. The Skyhawk was an ideal aircraft for a reserve pilot, being forgiving, reliable and fun to fly.

'Right from the *Model 5* briefing I resented the idea of being a part of such a huge "train" of jets flying over the frontline. I told my wingman that my intention was to break away from the "train", and I showed him on the map where we would leave the formation. I separated from the bulk of the aircraft bound for Syria and headed into the Yarmouk River valley. I flew very low along the latter as it routed us towards our target, and then I pulled up. We had been sent to bomb an SA-3 battery, and we were one of only two formations to hit their designated targets.

'This mission, coupled with my previous experiences from the Six Day War, galvanised my ideas on how things should be done during wartime. I also served as a fighting executive officer during the 1973 conflict, and my view was that all proposed missions had to be critically examined. On many occasions I asked for changes to be made. We instilled in the squadron a spirit of critical appraisal, and I think that this helped me survive the war. It also minimised No 115 Sqn's combat casualties.'

If *Challenge 4* had been a failure, *Model 5* was a disaster. The IDF/AF had not launched a pre-strike reconnaissance mission to pinpoint the exact location of the Syrian SAM batteries because there had not been time available to do so. Apparently, many of the mobile SAM batteries had been redeployed prior to *Model 5's* H-Hour, resulting in Israeli attack aircraft bombing empty sites. Post-mission, IDF intelligence concluded that only one SAM battery had been destroyed at a cost of six Phantom IIs shot down. Such an exchange ratio was unbearable, and the campaign to secure air superiority over Syria was immediately halted.

The IDF/AF failure on Day 2 meant grave consequences for the hard-pressed Skyhawk force. Until then, A-4 pilots flying into combat zones defended by SAMs had been motivated by their determination to support the troops under fire on the ground, whilst also hoping that air superiority would soon be achieved. The dismal results of *Challenge 4* and *Model 5* ended this hope, and left the Skyhawk squadrons badly exposed. CAS was essential but air superiority over both fronts was still not in hand. A-4 pilots would have to continue flying their missions against powerful and mostly intact networks of air defence assets.

Heavy attrition was now guaranteed, as the losses on Day 2 clearly showed. Ten Skyhawks were downed and only one pilot retrieved. Two jets had been lost during *Challenge 4* and four each during CAS missions over the Egyptian and Syrian fronts. Some 15 A-4s (nearly ten percent of the pre-war order of battle) had now been destroyed in just 48 hours. Many more had returned with varying degrees of battle damage.

The light attack units had provided critical air support for the beleaguered IDF regular divisions until the arrival of sizeable reserve forces both in the Golan Heights and in the Sinai. Together, IDF regular troops and IDF/AF pilots had stopped the Egyptian and Syrian advances.

From Day 3 onwards, the Skyhawks would support the reserves as they launched counteroffensives to push the enemy back on both fronts.

COUNTEROFFENSIVES

Two IDF reserve divisions reinforced each front and then launched a counteroffensive on Day 3. The Command South attack failed, however, and from 8 to 14 October the Egyptian front remained mostly static as both sides prepared for their next move. Command North enjoyed more success, except for in the Mount Hermon sector, and Syrian forces were slowly pushed back to the initial pre-war line. The IDF/AF had by now abandoned its plans for a large-scale air superiority battle, and the Skyhawks had to fly air support missions regardless of active AAA and SAM batteries that covered all altitudes over both fronts.

The air support plan for the morning of Day 3 was heavily influenced by the location of the various A-4 units. Squadrons based at Ramat David were tasked with flying air support over the Golan Heights, while Tel Nof-based units operated over the Suez Canal, with No 115 Sqn attacking bridges and No 116 Sqn performing CAS. The hazards of flying air support without air superiority became evident shortly after sunrise at 0539 hrs when two Skyhawks were lost, one over each front.

Up north, two A-4Es from No 110 Sqn had been tasked with attacking Syrian armour. The pilots involved could not positively identify valid targets, and as they were about to return home the wingman was hit by flak. He managed to jettison his external load and fly west so as to eject over Israeli territory, from where he was returned to Ramat David by helicopter. Down south, the first No 115 Sqn pair to depart Tel Nof on a bridge attack mission was Zvi Rozen and Itzhak Golan, who recalled;

'We pulled up to bomb and I saw two SAMs, one after the other, homing in on us. I yelled "Missiles, Break" and we broke away. Apparently, they were locked onto my wingman and shot him down. I saw his ejection, followed his parachute, reported and turned back for a second run on the target – a bridge across the southern sector of the Suez Canal north of Suez City.'

Rozen came down in enemy territory and became a PoW.

The 'fog of war' was still thick on Day 3, and Skyhawks flying CAS missions suffered accordingly. Confusion and uncertainty were so profound that a No 109 Sqn formation flying a racetrack pattern whilst awaiting the allocation of targets in the Golan Heights was ordered to fly a CAP over Ramat David. The jets flew to the Mediterranean, dumped their bombs and pretended to be interceptors for a while!

This was not an isolated case on the morning of Day 3. Later on, another pair of No 109 Sqn jets

Golden Eagle Squadron emergency posting pilot Yaniv Litani was on wartime temporary assignment to Squadron 116 from 6 October 1973. Litani safely returned the extensively damaged A-4E Skyhawk tail number 216 from an Operation *Model 5* AAA-suppression mission on 7 October 1973, but was killed two days later over the Egyptian front. (via author)

CHAPTER THREE

scrambled to attack naval vessels in the Mediterranean off Beirut, but found nothing except commercial shipping. Just before 1000 hrs, two more Skyhawks from No 109 Sqn launched to intercept enemy aircraft reportedly flying over northern Israel – none were in sight.

However, while this unit struggled to find the enemy in northern Israel, three more Skyhawks were lost over the Egyptian front. No 115 Sqn Operations Officer Zvika Bashan was killed while leading a four-ship formation on a CAS mission over a cloudy sector. Then two No 102 Sqn Skyhawks were lost, with one pilot retrieved and one killed.

The failure of the Command South counteroffensive triggered urgent pleas for air support, as IDF commanders feared that the Egyptians would try to exploit their success by renewing their attempts to advance deeper into Sinai. The IDF/AF was called in once again to halt the enemy's progress, and the hazardous nocturnal loft-bombing missions that followed mostly targeted Egyptian bridges across the Suez Canal. An exception was the attack on the IDF pier fortress at the southern end of the Suez Canal whilst Israeli troops were hiding inside bunkers. The fortress had been under siege by the enemy since 6 October, and it was finally seized by Egyptian forces nine days later.

The night of 8/9 October saw Syrian FROG (free rocket over ground) rockets target Ramat David, killing No 110 Sqn pilot David Dotan.

IDF/AF air support tactics were also analysed and adjusted at this point in the campaign. The lack of air superiority was a known fact, but the loss of 20 A-4s in 72 hours meant that changes had to be made for Day 4 in an attempt to curb this attrition. The fronts were duly divided up into four sectors (Golan Heights, Suez Canal north, Suez Canal centre and Suez Canal south). Each sector was assigned a light attack unit in the hope that pilots becoming better acquainted with the terrain would improve results and minimise losses. The basic pair also gave way to a three-ship formation, with the leader flying a loft pattern to suppress threats over the target while the trailing pair performed a dive-toss attack.

Six Skyhawks were lost, however, within three hours of the introduction of the three-ship tactic at sunrise on 9 October. The idea of a sector per squadron was a reasonable one, and the change to a three-ship formation showed a proactive adjustment to the harsh conditions facing pilots over the battlefield, but neither tactic solved the basic problem afflicting the A-4 unit – the lack of air superiority over the fronts. The IDF/AF's inability to suppress and destroy SAM and AAA batteries meant that the latter were free to exact a heavy toll on the light strike squadrons. The Skyhawks could not operate at medium altitude due to the SAM threat, and they were unable to survive the AAA and shoulder-launched SAMs at low altitude. Indeed, most A-4s downed in the conflict fell to flak or SA-7s, as the jet was relatively slow and lacked effective countermeasures.

Squadron 110's A-4E Skyhawk tail number 226 was lost in combat on the early morning hours of 8 October 1973. Flying wing to Squadron 110 reserve pilot Beni Zohar on a CAS mission over the Golan Heights, the Golden Eagle Squadron pilot on wartime temporary assignment to Squadron 110 ejected from Skyhawk 226 west of the Golan Heights, and was immediately picked up by a patrolling Bell 205 helicopter. Skyhawk 226 was photographed almost exactly two years before its demise when a Squadron 110 reserve pilot was traditionally 'baptized' after his Skyhawk solo in October 1971. (via author)

Three pilots were killed, two became PoWs and one was retrieved. Among those to die were two senior commanders. 'Smart 1' was usually the call-sign of No 116 Sqn CO Udi Shelach, but on the morning of Day 4 he was 'Smart 2', for he was flying lead for the dive-toss pair as part of the new three-ship tactic. The jets left Tel Nof at 0632 hrs to attack targets near the southern entrance to the Suez Canal. The lead A-4E loft-bombed as planned and then retreated to watch over the trailing pair. Smoke from an unidentified SAM (possibly an SA-3) was observed shortly after the dive-toss pair pulled up, and the missile homed in on 'Smart 2', which exploded in mid-air.

Confusion then followed, as 'Smart 1' correctly reported that 'Smart 2' had been lost. As previously mentioned, Shelach was always 'Smart 1', so for a while it appeared that the wingman had perished. Tel Nof Air Base commander Ran Ronen immediately realised what had happened, however, and prior to the return of the remaining 'Smart' Skyhawks, he had asked IDF/AF HQ for approval to install Phantom II pilot Shmulik Ben-Rom as the new CO of No 116 Sqn. Ronen's request was approved, and he informed Ben-Rom of the news as the latter was climbing out of his F-4E in a HAS on base after flying a mission over Egypt.

An hour later on the extreme northern flank of the Egyptian front, another senior commander flying as No 2 in a three-ship formation was lost. Ramat David's wing commander, Zorik Lev, had decided to fly a morning mission after the previous sleepless night, which had seen the deadly FROG attack. He was keen to lend support to the embattled No 110 Sqn in particular, as the unit had lost a pilot in the attack and two more in the air, as well as having had five jets shot down. A three-ship of Skyhawks duly launched and headed for the Port Said sector at the northern end of the Suez Canal. Confusion still surrounds the exact circumstances of Zorik Lev's loss, but his aircraft was last seen diving into the Mediterranean and he is still classified as missing in action.

Light attack units reverted to flying in pairs again towards noon, but losses continued and five more A-4s had been downed by sunset. Three were wingmen and two were pair leaders. One was killed, one made a PoW and three were retrieved. No 115 Sqn's Mario Shaked was the pilot to lose his life, as his formation leader Itzhak Golan recalls;

'In hindsight, Mario Shaked's behaviour during the mission briefing revealed his fatigue. I did not realise this at the time, but perhaps he sensed something. We flew a loft pattern and he disappeared. I did not see him get

A-4H Skyhawk tail number 04 (US Navy Bureau Number 155258) was lost in combat over the Egyptian front on 8 October 1973; the Squadron 102 pilot ejected and was retrieved. Skyhawk 04 was photographed at Hatzerim in May 1973 during the IDF/AF command handover parade when Moti Hod, IDF/AF commander from 1966 until 1973, handed over to Beni Peled, commander from 1973 until 1977. (via author)

One of the most symbolic photos of the Yom Kippur War is this image of an A-4E Skyhawk flying over IDF troops amidst typical Golan Heights terrain on 8 October 1973. (via author)

hit, as we flew one after the other, and he was behind me. I pulled out of my bombing run and called for him, but there was no answer. Following Shaked's loss our squadron initiated a change in tactics that saw one pilot committed to the loft-attack while the other watched over him. The roles would then change for the follow-up attack.'

No fewer than 11 Skyhawks had been shot down and many more had suffered varying degrees of battle damage while flying CAS missions on Day 4. Aside from the loss of No 116 Sqn CO Udi Shelach, his counterpart at No 110 Sqn had been hit in the back by a bullet during a CAS mission over the Golan Heights. And although the latter returned safely to Ramat David, his wound left him grounded.

By midnight on 9 October total Skyhawk losses stood at 31 jets – an average of nine per full fighting day. Compared to the then IDF/AF 'benchmark' figure from the Six Day War of almost two aircraft lost per fighting day per attack unit, this figure was high, but not extraordinarily so. The difference between the two conflicts lay in what had been accomplished to justify these losses. By the end of Day 4 of the Six Day War air superiority had been achieved and the armed forces of Egypt and Jordan defeated. The IDF/AF had failed to achieve air superiority by the end of Day 4 of the Yom Kippur War, while Israeli troops had barely stopped the Egyptians and were only now starting to repel the Syrians.

Air support was essential to IDF operations in line with pre-war doctrine and training. Yet Day 4 Skyhawk losses could not have been sustained should the war have continued over a longer timeframe. Therefore, CAS tactics had to be modified once again. The main obstacle preventing the IDF/AF from achieiving air superiority was the integrated network of SA-2, SA-3 and SA-6 SAM batteries on both fronts. But most A-4 losses up until then had been attributed to low-level AAA and shoulder-launched SAMs.

Despite the losses of Day 4, A-4 pilots noticed a decrease in the tempo of SAM launches. This was attributed to the depletion of missile stocks and the erosion of battery readiness due to continuous air strikes.

The low-level three-ship loft and dive-toss tactic was duly abandoned. Instead, A-4E/H units were ordered to operate from medium altitude, mostly in pairs. Interestingly, No 109 Sqn started Day 5 flying CAS missions from medium altitude in three-ship formations, but by noon the more usual pairs and four-ship formations had become the norm. The

Three 102 Squadron Skyhawks were lost in combat on the morning of 9 October 1973; the first of these was A-4H Skyhawk tail number 66. Initially a 115 Squadron aircraft, Skyhawk 66 was reissued during 1973 to the Flying School Fighter Advanced Training Squadron, from where it was assigned to 102 Squadron after the outbreak of war. Skyhawk 66 was photographed at Hatzerim in June 1973 after a minor mishap. (via author)

A-4Ns, which were slightly faster and more capable, continued to fly low-level loft missions mostly in pairs, but also in four-ship formations.

The unit sector tactic continued, but was not rigidly imposed. For example, on Day 5 No 115 Sqn flew over the Golan Heights in the morning and the Suez Canal in the afternoon, Nos 109 and 110 Sqns focused on Syria and No 116 Sqn flew over Port Said. Finally, No 102 Sqn had a day off due to heavy attrition, having lost 11 jets compared to No 109's five, No 110's six, No 115's five and No 116's four.

Another Day 5 innovation was No 116 Sqn's employment of AGM-62 Walleye TV-guided bombs, which were launched from medium altitude over the relatively safe air space of the Port Said sector. During the course of the day formations from Nos 115 and 116 Sqns were diverted from CAS missions to attack a SAM battery near Port Said. However, once on the scene the pilots determined that it was inoperable.

Medium-altitude operations had an adverse effect on bombing accuracy but positively affected pilot survivability, for they freed them from the principal threats of AAA and shoulder-launched SAMs. The primary danger at medium altitude was posed by SA-2, SA-3 and SA-6 SAMs, while MiGs were a lesser threat.

From Day 2, the Skyhawk pilots had encountered MiGs over the frontlines, but both sides focused on their primary missions and generally ignored each other. Sometimes, they were held and told to wait until enemy aircraft had been successfully cleared from the area by IDF/AF fighters. On Day 4, for example, two No 110 Sqn jets on a morning mission over the Golan Heights ran into 'MiGs', but the latter avoided engaging the A-4s and IDF/AF interceptors were vectored to the scene.

SA-2, SA-3 and SA-6 SAM batteries were still a danger to the air-support A-4s, but medium altitude operations offered more options when it came to taking evasive action. Following losses of Day 4, Day 5 was indeed a triumph for IDF/AF planners and Skyhawk pilots. They had jointly reacted to threats and implemented defensive tactics to negate them in almost real-time. As a result, just one jet was lost on 10 October 1973 – a Syrian SAM shot down a No 109 Sqn A-4H operating at medium altitude over the Golan Heights, killing Yehuda Ben-Ari. Despite this loss, medium-altitude attacks were now both encouraged and refined.

In yet another tactical innovation, TA-4Hs were tasked with flying continuous SAM launch patrols from the morning of Day 6 (11 October). They would spot missiles as they left their launchers and warn the threatened attack aircraft, therefore giving pilots more time to evade the impending threats.

The two losses on the morning of Day 4 were both 110 Squadron aircraft. The first was A-4E Skyhawk tail number 245, which was lost over the Golan Heights; the pilot ejected and was retrieved. Skyhawk 245 was photographed on 1 August 1973 after a ferry flight from Tel Nof to Etszion. (via author)

CHAPTER THREE

The second 102 Squadron combat loss of the morning of Day 4 involved A-4H Skyhawk tail number 50 (US Navy Bureau Number 155275), which was photographed in July 1972; the pilot of the destroyed Skyhawk became a prisoner of war in Egypt. (via author)

109 Squadron's emergency posting pilot Irik Baster was killed on a Day 7 morning loft mission over the Golan Heights. Baster flew lead to a four-ship formation when a SAM intercepted his A-4H Skyhawk, tail number 27. Skyhawk 27 was the sixth of 109 Squadron's 13 A-4 combat losses during the Yom Kippur War; six of these losses were aircraft flown as formation leaders and seven aircraft were lost while being flown as wingmen. (via author)

The air support plan for Day 6 prioritised operations in the Golan Heights, where the IDF offensive was gathering pace as it started to push the frontline towards Damascus. However, that morning the tempo of Syrian SAM launches increased once again, and soon after dawn No 115 Sqn (which had still been flying low-altitude, loft-attacks the previous day) lost two A-4Ns on its first two medium-altitude attack missions over the northern sector of the Golan Heights.

This prompted a swift return to low-altitude operations – mostly loft and delayed dive-toss attacks. The TA-4 SAM launch detection patrols were maintained, however, with the back seat observer usually being a senior pilot. Also from Day 6, the two-seat Skyhawks were assigned to fly artillery-spotting missions, with a gunnery officer in the back seat.

All six A-4 losses on 11 October came over the Golan Heights during both medium- and low-altitude operations, with one pilot being killed and five captured. Mixed attack patterns, from medium and low altitude, continued on the 12th, although the previous day's concentration of force over the Golan Heights was no longer required. The air support provided by the two Ramat David Skyhawk squadrons was considered adequate, with midland and southern-based A-4 units operating almost exclusively over the Egyptian front. Among these, the two Tel Nof squadrons' main sector of the day was Port Said, whilst the A-4Ns of No 115 Sqn mostly attacked SAM batteries with cluster bomb units (CBUs) whilst the A-4Es of No 116 Sqn flew CAS.

Up north, the Ramat David units lost two more aircraft to Syrian SAMs. No 109 Sqn four-ship leader Irik Baster was killed during a morning dive-toss mission, and at noon a No 110 Sqn four-ship leader ejected over Israeli territory.

Fierce fighting during Days 7 and 8 did not result in significant breakthroughs. The IDF advance towards Damascus had been halted and a counterattack by an Iraqi expeditionary force was eventually contained by 13 October. Exchanges of fire and small-scale local offensives in Sinai continued as both sides prepared to launch large-scale offensives.

IDF success in the north prompted Syria to commit an operational army reserve and more air power to the fight. Air strikes by MiG-17s and Su-7s intensified, and their interception over the frontline by Israeli fighters was an extremely hazardous business because of Syrian integrated AAA and SAM threats. In order to suppress these air strikes, the IDF/AF decided to step up its attacks on Syrian air bases, and A-4Ns were assigned to this campaign on the morning of 13 October.

The Skyhawk force was to provide air support over both fronts, attacking SAM batteries east of the Golan Heights and participating in airfield strikes in Syria. Naturally, the squadrons based at Hatzerim and Ramat David were assigned CAS missions over both the southern and northern fronts, respectively, while No 115 Sqn's A-4Ns bombed SyAAF air bases. This left the A-4Es of No 116 Sqn to attack Syrian SAMs.

Morning air support over the Golan Heights cost the IDF/AF two Skyhawks, both from No 109 Sqn. The wingman of a pair of jets flying a loft-bomb attack against Iraqi forces was shot down and captured. An hour later, a four-ship formation attacked in pairs from medium altitude over the same sector. The tactic adopted on this occasion was that while one pair bombed, the second pair watched for SAMs, after which they exchanged roles. In this case, the TA-4 observation aircraft and both the watching and attacking pairs all saw the SAM launches, but a missile still shot down the leader of the formation. The pilot ejected over no-man's land amidst a tank battle and quickly met up with friendly forces.

Meanwhile, the aviators of Nos 115 and 116 Sqns prepared to attack airfields and SAM batteries, respectively. Time-over-target for the attack

102 Squadron suffered three combat losses during medium-altitude morning operations over the Golan Heights, with all three pilots becoming PoWs in Syria. One of the three lost aircraft was A-4 Skyhawk tail number 08 (US Navy Bureau Number 155260) that had served in 102 Squadron since 1968 and was photographed in November 1972 after a minor accident at Hatzerim. (via author)

The third 102 Squadron combat loss of the morning of 9 October 1973 was A-4H Skyhawk tail number 90, which was photographed pre-war beside a 105 Squadron improved Super Mystere. The different nozzle contours of the two J52-powered attack aircraft are clearly visible in this view. This structural difference motivated the Skyhawk's 'Barrel' modification project (see page 60) that was launched during the closing stages of the Yom Kippur War. (via author)

CHAPTER THREE

Another of the Golden Eagle Squadron's aircraft lost during the Yom Kippur War was A-4E Skyhawk tail number 257, which was photographed at Etszion in August 1973 during a turnaround exercise loaded with 500-lb Mark 82 bombs in 'direct slinging' under the wing stations. Skyhawk 257 was among the group of Golden Eagle Squadron aircraft and pilots on wartime temporary assignment to 110 Squadron at Ramat David from 6 October 1973. Flying in the lead of a four-ship formation that departed Ramat David at 1340 on 12 October 1973, tasked to fly air support over the Golan Heights, Skyhawk 257 became the victim of a Syrian SAM. The pilot managed to fly west until obliged to eject over Israeli territory, so that only 30 minutes after take-off from Ramat David, the injured pilot was at a forward medical evacuation airfield waiting for the next transport aircraft flying to hospital in midland Israel. (via author)

mission on the MiG-17 base at Damascus Elmaza, was 0715 hrs. The lead four-ship formation suppressed the base's air defences through loft attacks with CBUs, while the second formation targeted the runway in a series of dive-toss strikes with general purpose bombs. Finally, the third four-ship dropped CBUs over the base's dispersal areas. The No 115 Sqn attack on Elmaza was deemed to have been a success, with IDF intelligence reporting that it was inactive for three hours.

Following the failure of *Challenge 4* and *Model 5*, the IDF/AF avoided large-scale attacks on Egyptian and Syrian air defences. However, it continuously targeted their network of SAM batteries through pinpoint attacks on specific sites. F-4Es flew most of these missions, with A-4s operating in a support role. An IDF intelligence evaluation in preparation for the morning missions on Day 8 stated that the Syrian SAM battery network east of the Golan Heights had been battered but was still active.

One SA-2 and three SA-3 batteries were to be attacked on the morning of 13 October. The Ramat David Skyhawk squadrons were tasked with flying AGM-12 and AGM-45 stand-off suppression patrols, while No 116 Sqn sortied a 'killer' four-ship formation that would be orbiting at medium altitude ready to attack active batteries.

Skyhawks flying stand-off missions also fell victim to enemy air defences, and that morning a No 102 Sqn TA-4 was lost (one of two downed on the 13th). The No 102 Sqn jet was on a morning visual reconnaissance mission east of the Suez Canal with an intelligence officer observing from the back seat. The TA-4 headed north at 30,000 ft, and early into its mission it was targeted by at least three SA-2s whilst opposite the southern sector of the Suez Canal. The first two missiles streaked past the Skyhawk, but the third exploded close enough to send the jet spinning to earth. Both the crewmen ejected, but pilot Ran Ofri was killed. The injured observer landed safely within Israeli-held territory.

There was little fighting in the Golan Heights for the rest of Day 8, allowing the Ramat David squadrons to enjoy a relatively quiet Sunday. Northern-based A-4s flew observation and patrols, but most aircraft tasked with performing CAS were not called on to attack targets.

Attention shifted south to Sinai, where the Egyptians finally renewed their offensive. This time the Israelis were ready, with IDF armour claiming 200 enemy tanks destroyed, which in turn caused the Egyptian offensive to falter. The southern A-4E/H squadrons flew air support over Sinai, with No 116 Sqn expending plenty of AGM-62 Walleye TV-guided bombs against Egyptian armour.

No 115 Sqn was also assigned air support missions over Sinai, but these were flown only after pilots had completed their morning tasking – an attack on the EAF air base at Salhiya. This was a major raid involving eight Skyhawks and a similar number of Phantom IIs. Their objective was to neutralise Salhiya, from where MiG-17s operated, therefore denying air support operations from the base during the critical battle in Sinai.

The lead F-4E formation was tasked with SEAD over Salhiya, the trailing Phantom II formation bombed runways and the Skyhawks struck HASs. MiG-21s defended the base, intercepting the trailing Skyhawks. A brief air combat ensued, but the Skyhawks disengaged safely as IDF/AF interceptors bounced the MiG-21s and claimed four kills.

The impact of the Day 9 air base attack on Salhiya was rated as overwhelming by IDF intelligence, the strike being arguably the most effective airfield attack mission of the entire conflict. Salhiya was reportedly inactive for several days after the attack, with flight operations eventually resuming on 21 October.

The successful blunting of the Egyptian offensive on 14 October gave Israel an opportunity to launch a counteroffensive of its own in Sinai. The IDF chose to form a wedge between the Egyptian 2nd Army in the north and 3rd Army in the south. This wedge would in turn create a corridor through which IDF forces could push forward towards the Suez Canal just north of Great Bitter Lake. There, Israeli troops would cross the canal and form a bridgehead at Deversoir from where IDF divisions could advance south and southwest to smash the vulnerable rear echelons of the Egyptian army, threaten to move on Cairo and eventually encircle the entire Egyptian 3rd Army.

The IDF plan had been made possible not only because of the failure of the Egyptian offensive on the 14th but also because of the hard-won air superiority achieved by the IDF/AF east of the frontline.

The IDF's Command South committed two divisions to the Deversoir offensive, leaving only modest forces (less than two divisions) behind in Sinai to face two Egyptian armies. It knew it could do this because the Egyptians realised that any attempt to advance exposed their armoured formations to deadly Israeli air strikes. The vision of lurking A-4s pouncing on hapless tanks advancing beyond their AAA and SAM shield deterred numerically superior Egyptian forces from further offensive action, thus allowing the IDF to launch the Suez Canal crossing manoeuvre.

On 15 October IDF/AF attack aircraft were kept busy supporting fierce fighting along the soon-to-be-established corridor to Deversoir. Between 13 and 15 October the

Two-seat Skyhawks flew attack and observation missions during the Yom Kippur War. Several TA-4s were lost in attack missions but only TA-4H Skyhawk tail number 43 was lost while engaged in an observation mission east of the Egyptian front on 13 October 1973. Skyhawk 43 was originally a 116 Squadron aircraft, later issued to 102 Squadron, and then Flying School Fighter Advanced Training Squadron from October 1972. It was photographed at Hatzerim in November 1972. (via author)

The first Israeli Skyhawk, A-4H number 5301 (US Navy Bureau Number 155242) did not survive the war. 109 Squadron's Skyhawk 01 was shot down over the Golan Heights on the morning of 13 October 1973. The pilot ejected and was retrieved. Skyhawk 01 was photographed in July 1970 after a turnaround competition, loaded with six 500-lb Mk 82 bombs on MERs, two external fuel tanks and two rocket pods. (via author)

CHAPTER THREE

The two Day 10 Skyhawk combat losses were a pair from 109 Squadron that departed Ramat David at 1500 hrs, tasked to fly air support over the Golan Heights. Both were shot down; the leader was retrieved but his wingman Gabi Saar, flying A-4H Skyhawk tail number 52, was killed. (via author)

tactical situation on the two fronts had switched. The Syrian front changed from being dynamic to mostly static, while the Egyptian front was transformed into a mobile battlefield.

Obviously, these changes had a significant impact on the mission tasking of the Skyhawk force. Operations over the Golan Heights continued, but the emphasis shifted south to the Egyptian front. And although the Syrian front became a secondary theatre in many respects, the Golan Heights remained a dangerous and hostile war zone. As if to prove this point, both Skyhawk losses on Day 10 (15 October) occurred in the north. A pair of No 109 Sqn A-4s that had departed Ramat David at 1500 hrs flew low over a concentration of Syrian AAA batteries and were both hit. The lead pilot managed to steer his aircraft out to sea, where he ejected – a rescue helicopter soon retrieved him. His wingman, Gabi Saar, was killed, however.

No Skyhawk losses were sustained over the Egyptian front, despite several jets returning home with battle damage. Whenever possible, the A-4s flew at a medium altitude, which was above the enemy's SAM engagement envelope. By then all Skyhawk squadrons had seen a lot of action, and each unit had developed a range of mission 'specialties' when it came to weapon employment. No 116 Sqn, for example, used the AGM-62 Walleye to hunt down Egyptian tanks, while No 115 Sqn excelled in air base strikes and flying loft attack patterns.

The successful air base attack mission on Salhiya on 14 October was followed by a similar strike on Kotamiya the following day. The plan of attack and force composition were generally similar, except that four four-ship formations of Skyhawks were involved on this occasion. Once again, IDF intelligence rated the mission extremely successful. Monitoring Egyptian activity, it concluded that Kotamiya was inactive until the late afternoon of 16 October.

CANAL CROSSING

Israeli paratroopers used rubber boats to cross the Suez Canal on the night of 15/16 October, thus establishing the Deversoir bridgehead. The Day 11 air support plan assigned four Skyhawk squadrons to the south, leaving just No 109 Sqn operating over the Golan Heights.

Most Skyhawk missions over the corridor and bridgehead involved loft-bombing with CBUs and general-purpose ordnance. This method of attack had to be employed as the whole area was still within range of active Egyptian SAM batteries. But flying low exposed the A-4s to a wall of AAA and shoulder-launched SAMs. The slow, heavily loaded Skyhawks lacked efficient self-defence systems, making them extremely vulnerable to both threats. Yet the A-4 was a robust war machine, and many returned with heavily holed tail sections and bad hydraulic leaks.

While the Skyhawks focused on providing air support over Deversoir, F-4Es were tasked with flying a SEAD mission in the Port Said sector at noon. No 115 Sqn was also assigned to this effort, and the unit also bombed a nearby Egyptian barracks following the strike. The Port Said action was, however, a sideshow to the main event at Deversoir. By noon the Egyptians had realised that the Israeli action was not a daring local commando raid but a strategically significant offensive. Reserves were hastily mobilised and more air power was committed to the battle.

Shortly after 1400 hrs, a No 102 Sqn Skyhawk was lost over Deversoir. 'Amper' section had been tasked to attack targets in the Kantara sector, but it had been diverted in flight to Deversoir. The four Skyhawks attacked but 'Amper 1' vanished from sight after bombing, killing reserve pilot Menachem Eyal.

All five Skyhawk units headed south on 17 October, and as per the day before, most sorties took the form of CAS missions over Deversoir. Yet, the IDF/AF's major operation on Day 12 of the war was the suppression of Egyptian SAM batteries west of the IDF bridgehead. The Skyhawk squadrons' contribution was minor – four No 115 Sqn aircraft releasing Tal-3 decoys prior to the onslaught by Phantom IIs.

The IDF bridgehead across the Suez Canal was then still only a small sector for the whole Skyhawk force to operate in. Therefore, just Nos

102 Squadron's section leader, call sign AMPER, was reserve pilot Menachem Eyal. The AMPER four-ship formation was tasked to fly an air support mission over the IDF bridgehead corridor east of the Suez Canal sometime after 1400 hrs on 16 October 1973, but AMPER 1 did not return to Hatzerim; A-4H Skyhawk tail number 51 (US Navy Bureau Number 155276) was lost in combat, and pilot Menachem Eyal was killed. This photo of Skyhawk 51 was taken in June 1971 after a turnaround competition held as part of 102 Squadron's third anniversary celebrations. (via author)

102 and 115 Sqns flew CAS over Deversoir, with Nos 109, 110 and 116 Sqns hitting targets in the Ismailiya, Kantara and Port Said sectors, respectively.

Two Skyhawks were lost minutes after 1100 hrs. The first to go down was a No 110 Sqn jet that was leading a pair of aircraft on a loft-bombing mission in the Kantara sector. Reserve pilot Maoz Poraz was killed. A short while later a No 102 Sqn aircraft was shot down over the Deversoir sector, but this time the pilot ejected safely and was retrieved by a rescue helicopter.

These losses prompted the withdrawal of the Ramat David squadrons from the Sinai front. The Ismailiya and Kantara sectors were not crucial to ground operations at this time, so from 1200 hrs Nos 109 and 110 Sqn had a break from frontline operations.

No 116 Sqn operations over Port Said continued, however, the unit keeping up its harassment of the air defence network in this mostly isolated sector. Flying missions in this theatre usually posed few risks to A-4 pilots, but at 1200 hrs on 17 October MiG-21 pilots intercepted Skyhawks over Port Said. At this point a TA-4 observer and two attack pairs were operating over the Port Said, and the Egyptian fighters went for one of the latter. No 'proper' air combat followed, the four MiG-21s making do with a single air-to-air missile pass, although this was sufficient to damage the lead Skyhawk. As was often the case in the early days of air-to-air missile technology, the aircraft emerged from the explosion with only minor damage and was able to return to base. The Skyhawks' confrontation with MiG-21s over Port Said was, in fact, the prelude to a major air battle. By noon, No 116 Sqn had flown 37 sorties (three observation and 17 attack pairs) over the Port Said sector, at which point No 115 Sqn took over. It flew ten more prior to sunset at 1708 hrs.

On Day 13 No 115 Sqn had the morning off, No 102 Sqn was assigned the Port Said sector, No 116 Sqn mostly flew CAS over the Deversoir bridgehead and Nos 109, 110 and 116 Sqns were committed to Operation *Cracker 22* – the renewing of the offensive against Egypt's SAM batteries.

By 16 October IDF intelligence stated that SAM batteries deployed in the Port Said sector had been effectively neutralised. With the Israeli offensive west of the Suez Canal gathering pace, the IAF was ordered to target surviving SAM sites in the area so as to secure air superiority over the bridgehead and ensure proper air support for the IDF divisions as they advanced into Egypt.

IDF/AF planners decided to divide the Egyptian air defence network up into segments, attacking one at a time from north to south. The northernmost active segment, south of Port Said, was the Kantara array,

Inside the hangar of the Hatzerim Wing Maintenance Squadron's Skyhawk workshop during the Yom Kippur War, repairing battle-damaged aircraft. The aircraft in the background is A-4H Skyhawk tail number 67, which was damaged on a Day 11 afternoon air support mission over the Egyptian front. 102 Squadron pilot Amos Yadlin flew wingman in Skyhawk 67 to attack Egyptian armour with five Rockeye cluster bomb units. Both Skyhawks suffered SA-7 damage and Yadlin made an emergency landing at Refidim. Two days later, Yadlin ferried Skyhawk 67 with a temporary fix from Refidim to Hatzerim, where the aircraft was repaired. (via author)

where IDF intelligence identified six SA-2 and SA-3 SAM batteries, plus the possible 'ambush' deployment of mobile SA-6s. The attacking force was divided into support, suppression and destruction elements. No 116 Sqn was part of the suppression force, while Nos 109 and 110 Sqns provided the second, third and fourth waves of the destruction force.

The first Skyhawks to depart on a *Cracker 22* mission were four No 116 Sqn pairs. Each of the eight A-4Es was armed with three CBUs, and they had been tasked with flying loft-bomb attacks so as to suppress AAA scattered among the Kantara SAM batteries.

The Ramat David Skyhawks followed in three waves. Each unit sent in three pairs per wave for a total force of 36 Skyhawks. Six pairs flew in each wave, with each pair tasked to bomb a single SAM battery. The jets approached the Kantara sector at low altitude in three 'trailer' formations, with a No 109 Sqn A-4H pairing flying lead with two No 110 Sqn A-4Es following. Equipped with the Crystal weapon delivery and navigation system, the No 109 Sqn Skyhawks shepherded the No 110 Sqn jets to the initial point, where the pairs separated. They then flew a different course on their final legs towards their individual targets, which were attacked in a delayed dive-toss bombing pattern.

Time-over-target for the first Phantom II wave was 0930 hrs, and two F-4Es were lost. The 12 Skyhawks of the second wave followed, but a No 109 Sqn pair were exposed to an SA-6 ambush immediately after pop-up and had to abort their attack – the formation leader landed his damaged Skyhawk at Refidim, in Sinai.

The remaining two No 109 Sqn pairs attacked as planned, but came under a massive SAM attack during their retreat. A wingman's Skyhawk exploded in mid-air, killing Gershon Fonk. Similarly, a No 110 Sqn leader's Skyhawk was shot down during the disengagement phase, forcing Gideon Sharon to eject – he was taken prisoner. A second No 109 Sqn Skyhawk was lost during the third wave pop-up, and the pilot who ejected over no-man's land was rescued by IDF troops.

Two more A-4s suffered substantial battle damage, with the leader of a fourth wave pair from No 109 Sqn being forced to land at Hatzerim. However, a No 110 Sqn wingman lost control of his damaged jet on final approach to Ramat David and he had to eject. The pilot survived, but the Skyhawk killed four IDF/AF personnel when it crashed.

Cracker 22 was considered successful, with IDF intelligence reporting that the Kantara SAM batteries had been destroyed. Six aircraft had been lost, however – one jet downed per SAM battery claimed destroyed.

A pair of 102 Squadron Skyhawks prepares to depart Hatzerim on 18 October 1973. The lead Skyhawk, tail number 22, is loaded with ten 500-lb Mk 82 bombs, six attached to a MER under the fuselage and four under the wing. The wingman, Skyhawk tail number 55, is armed with five cluster bomb units (three attached to under-fuselage TERs and two loaded onto the inner wing stations), and two Mk 82 bombs on the outboard wing stations. (via author)

CHAPTER THREE

109 Squadron's A-4H Skyhawk 99 (US Navy Bureau Number 157920) was an Operation *Cracker 22* combat loss; pilot Gershon Fonk was killed on an SA-2 attack mission on 18 October 1973. Fonk was flying wingman in a second-wave pair that successfully bombed its assigned target, an SA-2 battery in the Kantara sector. During disengagement the Skyhawks were rather slow, around 250 knots, and quite vulnerable at an altitude of 4,000 feet over a still-active hostile air defense. The Skyhawks were already flying east of the Suez Canal when two SAMs, most likely SA-2s, intercepted the pair from their rear hemisphere. The leader managed to evade 'his' missile but the other missile struck Skyhawk 99. (via author)

Simultaneously, IDF armoured formations captured Egyptian SAM batteries west of the Deversoir bridgehead and reported the destruction of three or four installations. Under this cumulative offensive, the Egyptian air defence force began to crumble, and proper air support was at last within the grasp of IDF units.

This situation was fully exploited the next day, 19 October. Skyhawk force operations focused on the Deversoir bridgehead as the jets supported the IDF, and targets were also struck in the Kantara sector following the success of *Cracker 22*. Sorties were also flown over the Golan Heights, significantly against Jordanian troops that had reinforced the Syrian front, as well as strikes on Mount Hermon.

The Kantara sector was initially assigned to No 109 Sqn, which flew 42 sorties from morning till noon. The Tel Nof Skyhawk units operated over Deversoir, but by the late morning hours Nos 115 and 116 Sqns had also been tasked with attacking targets within the Kantara sector. Both squadrons continued operations over Deversoir, so several missions were changed in mid-air from Kantara to Deversoir, or vice-versa. This was partially because of a renewed offensive by Egyptian air power over the IDF bridgehead – at least three major attack waves came in between noon and dusk. Each time Egyptian attack aircraft and escorting fighters appeared over the Deversoir sector, IDF/AF interceptors were vectored in to engage them and A-4s flying CAS missions were hastily diverted away from the bridgehead area.

No 116 Sqn had continued to fly several AGM-62 Walleye missions per day during this period. The weapon's principal targets were Egyptian tanks, but none were available for two A-4s on a noon mission over the Kantara sector on the 19th. They flew the usual racetrack pattern as they waited for orders from the air liaison officer. Running low on fuel, the pilots faced the dilemma of either attacking 'something' or returning to base. The latter was not considered to be a desirable option, so the air liaison officer ordered the pair to attack trenches. Such fortifications were not ideal targets for the AGM-62, but they attacked as ordered, and also made a strafing pass.

Strafing was generally banned by then, as such passes were extremely hazardous and exposed attack aircraft to flak and shoulder-launched SAMs that, as already indicated, had inflicted most of the IDF/AF's losses in the war to date. Strafing was little used, therefore, and it was certainly not encouraged. The leader of the aforementioned pair was duly reprimanded during the end-of-day squadron debrief.

No Skyhawk losses on Day 14 validated the significance of air superiority. Accumulated experience, evolving tactics and the implementation of lessons hard-learned over the past two weeks also contributed. Obviously, there was a positive connection between Operation *Cracker 22* on 18 October and the loss-free Skyhawk operations over the Kantara sector on Day 14, as well as between IDF armoured attacks on Egyptian SAM batteries west of Deversoir and more successful A-4 missions over the bridgehead theatre on 19 October.

IDF/AF planners keen to achieve total air superiority over eastern Egypt now shifted their focus from north to south, and the SAM batteries in the Ismailiya sector. Operation *Cracker 23* targeted these on the morning of 20 October, this mission being primarily a Phantom II affair. Skyhawks continued to fly their CAS missions, however, although the Egyptian defences were now much less of a threat. Nevertheless, there were still plenty of mobile and shoulder-launched SAMs in the area, and aviators had to remain on their guard.

Beyond refined attack patterns and improved evasive tactics, Skyhawk pilots began to release chaff bundles against radar-guided SAMs. Eventually, flares would also be added to chaff dispensers to defeat heat-seeking SAMs as well, but they were not available during the Yom Kippur War. Skyhawk anti-heat-seeking SAM countermeasures were hastily introduced, however, during the closing stages of the Yom Kippur War.

During 1968, the IDF/AF had launched a Super Mystere upgrade programme that included powerplant replacement, the French Atar 101 giving way to the American Pratt & Whitney J52. One in a long list of reasons for such a swap was commonality with the J52-powered Skyhawk, then entering service as the Super Mystere replacement. In order to fit the J52 into the French attack aircraft, major structural modifications had to be made primarily because of the differing dimensions and weight of the two powerplants. The French engine was also equipped with afterburner and the J52 was not. The nozzle of the improved Super Mystere had to be reshaped with a longer tailpipe that ended well aft of the tail section's vertical and horizontal flying surfaces.

During the Yom Kippur War, improved Super Mysteres and Skyhawks flew similar missions and faced identical threats. Yet, the improved Super Mystere suffered fewer losses and less damage to heat-seeking SA-7s. Wartime analysis of this phenomenon indicated that the

The two Ramat David-based Skyhawk squadrons lost two aircraft each during Operation *Cracker 22*, the suppression and destruction of enemy air defences on 18 October 1973. 110 Squadron's first loss was A-4E Skyhawk tail number 253 (US Bureau Number 152032) that flew lead in a pair tasked to attack a SAM battery. The pair bombed as planned but during disengagement the leader's Skyhawk 253 was hit and he had to eject. This was his second Yom Kippur War ejection; the first was from A-4E Skyhawk tail number 245 over the Syrian front on 9 October 1973. In this second wartime ejection, the pilot was less lucky and was not retrieved, but was taken prisoner in Egypt. (via author)

Two damaged 109 Squadron Skyhawks landed at forward air bases in the wake of Operation *Cracker 22* on 18 October 1973. The second Skyhawk emergency landing involved a fourth-wave pair leader tasked to revisit an SA-2 battery. During disengagement the rather slow Skyhawks were most vulnerable to SA-7s and, indeed, one of these shoulder-launched weapons ripped the tail section from the Skyhawk. Many warning lights came on in the cockpit, and the pilot was sure that ejection was only a matter of timing. However, to his amazement the Skyhawk responded to control inputs and the fire warning light went out. Escorted by his wingman, an emergency landing was planned at El Arish but the experienced reserve pilot flying as wingman encouraged his leader to continue flying to Hatzerim, which was better equipped to handle, and eventually photograph, such an emergency. (via author)

modified tail-pipe of the improved Super Mystere kept the explosion of the missile's proximity-fused warhead away from the vital parts of the jet. This slight shift farther back from the missile's normal 'hot' aiming point actually made the difference when it came to the survivability of the two aircraft.

The A-4's nozzle ended well ahead of the tail section's vertical and horizontal flying surfaces, so when a missile's proximity fuse exploded the warhead slightly behind the nozzle, the resulting fragments sprayed the Skyhawk's tail section, holing the flying surfaces and puncturing the crucial hydraulic fluid pipes.

A suggestion from the field triggered No 22 Air Maintenance Unit at Tel Nof to design a tailpipe modification for the Skyhawk. It came up with a nozzle extension that in plan view ended behind the rear of the tail section's vertical and horizontal flying surfaces, as with the improved Super Mystere. The modification was hastily designed and No 22 Air Maintenance Unit prepared a prototype installation. Flight Test Centre pilots then made four flights in the modified Skyhawk within 24 hours and cleared the modification for squadron service. Within a further 24 hours the modification was operational.

Colloquially known among IAF ranks as the 'Barrel', the first Skyhawk destined to be fitted with this modification was flown from Tel Nof to the Israel Aircraft Industries facility at Lod Airport on the evening of 20 October. The 'Barrel'-modified A-4N was returned to No 115 Sqn the following morning.

MOUNT HERMON

The Yom Kippur War was now clearly drawing to a close. Egypt and Syria were struggling to preserve territorial achievements before the expected ceasefire came into effect. Israel, on the other hand, was striving to abolish Syrian territorial gains in the north while maximising IDF territorial gains in the south. The Skyhawk force supported both efforts on 21 October, with the northern-based Skyhawk squadrons operating over the Golan Heights and the remaining light strike units flying over the Egyptian front.

The Tel Nof A-4 squadrons flew nearly 100 CAS sorties on this day, with No 115 Sqn working mostly with IDF divisions west of the Suez Canal, chiefly in the Fayid sector. No 116 Sqn's main effort was bombing Egyptian 2nd Army assets east of the Suez Canal in the Ismailiya sector. By now the Egyptian air defence force had been shattered, allowing IDF/AF interceptors to establish a hunting ground for enemy aircraft overhead the IDF bridgehead. Israeli attack aircraft were now also free to operate primarily from medium altitudes, being safe from SAM threats and enemy interceptors.

Up north, the hot spot of Day 16 was Mount Hermon, which was the the only pre-war Israeli-held territory still in Syrian control. The entire Golan Heights to the south, Lebanon to the west and Syria to the east were within view from the summit of Mount Hermon, hence its strategic importance. IDF Operation *Dessert* was launched on 21 October in an effort to retake the fortified observation post atop Mount Hermon.

The Ramat David Skyhawks softened up Syrian positions in the Mount Hermon sector from late morning until sunset. Generally flying at medium altitude, the Skyhawks went about their business without interruption, except for occasional warnings of SAM launches or enemy interceptors approaching the area. SAMs did not threaten the A-4s, and whenever SyAAF fighters appeared over Mount Hermon, the Skyhawk pilots were ordered to temporarily withdraw until the danger was over. Nevertheless, a jet was lost over Mount Hermon on the 21st.

A No 109 Sqn four-ship formation departed Ramat David at 1105 hrs tasked with bombing the road leading to the fortification atop the mountain. Loaded with CBUs, the Skyhawks operated in pairs, with one bombing from medium altitude while the other watched out for threats. The pairs then switched roles. Shortly after the lead pair had completed their bombing pattern, the leader's wingman, Eitan Lahav, dived into the ground and was killed. The post-war report from the IDF/AF central command and control post linked this loss to a Syrian SAM ambush. Squadron reports indicated that no missile launches were noted, however, and there was no flak seen either. The loss was therefore attributed by No 109 Sqn to some sort of disorientation.

Operation *Dessert* concluded with Israeli success, IDF infantry reoccupying the Mount Hermon summit fortification at 1030 hrs on the morning of 22 October.

The No 109 Sqn jet downed over Mount Hermon was the 53rd Israeli Skyhawk to be lost during the Yom Kippur War. Fortunately for the IDF/AF, the US government had agreed to make good combat aircraft losses through an emergency aid scheme. Phantom IIs and Skyhawks were flown to Israel, with the first A-4s that landed at Tel Nof on 21 October being issued to No 110 Sqn at Ramat David that same evening.

The emergency aid Skyhawks were A-4E/Fs drawn from active and reserve duty US Navy and US Marine Corps squadrons in a 'one-per-one' replacement ratio for IDF/AF A-4E/H losses that totalled 46 aircraft. The seven A-4Ns that had been destroyed were replaced by new-production aircraft that increased the overall Israeli N-model buy to 117 jets. The US Naval Air Rework Facility at Norfolk, in Virginia, prepared the A-4E/Fs for delivery to Israel, and experienced American Skyhawk pilots were asked to volunteer to perform the ferry flights.

A US Air Force KC-135 tanker shepherded and refuelled the Skyhawks on the first leg of the five-hour flight to the Azores. With the tanker then returning to the US, the Skyhawks made a night stop in the Azores. Portugal was the only European nation offering assistance to the US for the airlift to Israel, so the next leg would far more complicated. The Skyhawks departed the Azores and trailed a US Navy Reserve KA-3 tanker. Off the Spanish coast, a US Marine Corps KC-130 tanker briefly took over for final fuel top up prior to the Skyhawks entering the airspace over the Mediterranean Sea. The jets flew on from here without a lead ship.

115 Squadron's A-4N Skyhawk tail number 376 taxis at Tel Nof upon its return from a Yom Kippur War mission. The 115 Squadron aircraft used AIM-9B and AIM-9D Sidewinder air-to-air missiles for self-defence, usually carrying only one missile to enable the aircraft to carry the maximum offensive ordnance possible. Skyhawk 376 was ferried from Tel Nof to Lod on the evening of 20 October 1973 and returned to Tel Nof the following morning complete with the 'Barrel' modification, the first A-4N with an extended nozzle for added protection against SA-7 shoulder-launched missiles. (via author)

More than five hours after take-off from the Azores, the Skyhawks homed onto the TACAN beacon of the aircraft carrier USS *Franklin D Roosevelt* (CV-42) and landed aboard the vessel for a second night stop. The third leg of the ferry flight was made the following day, when the Skyhawks were catapulted from *Roosevelt* and headed east for Israel.

Flying into a war zone, the Skyhawks had their guns loaded with ammunition, but the US Navy pilots had no idea where exactly they were headed! The plan was to rendezvous with Israeli fighters, and they would in turn lead the Skyhawks into land. This evolution worked as planned, with the escorted A-4s landing at Tel Nof. The American pilots spent the night here without ever being told the name of the base that they were staying at, prior to boarding a USAF transport aircraft heading home.

These emergency aid Skyhawks were hastily repainted in IDF/AF colours and issued to squadrons. By then, however, the initial high rate of attrition that had worried Israeli leaders and IDF commanders to the extent that emergency aid requests had been made to the US government had diminished. The IDF/AF had achieved air superiority over the fronts, modified attack tactics and implemented lessons learned from losses and failures so that Skyhawk combat attrition was down from 31 aircraft on Days 1 to 4 to 21 aircraft from Days 5 to 13 and only one Skyhawk lost from Days 14 to 19.

FIRST CEASEFIRE

Following the battle for Mount Hermon, the United Nations Security Council issued Resolution 338 calling for a ceasefire in the Middle East within 12 hours, effective by 1900 hrs on the evening of 22 October 1973. Skyhawk pilots attending morning squadron-level briefings were informed that a ceasefire had indeed been agreed, so the next few hours would probably be the last of the war. This information prompted a maximum effort, with No 115 Sqn launching 74 sorties on the 22nd. This set a unit-level record.

No 109 Sqn continued flying CAS missions over Mount Hermon from sunrise until the bloody battle came to an end during the late morning.

Combat-loss replacement Skyhawks began arriving at Tel Nof from 21 October 1973, following a long flight from the USA. Reportedly, some 30 of the 46 replacement airframes flew 85 operational sorties before the ceasefire. (via author)

Emergency aid A-4E Skyhawk US Navy Bureau Number 150034 being hastily repainted at night inside a Ramat David Wing Maintenance Squadron hangar. (via author)

From noon No 109 Sqn joined the other Skyhawk units that had been fiercely attacking Egyptian targets from shortly after dawn. Their primary target was the Egyptian 3rd Army east of the Suez Canal, and they also supported IDF divisions west of the Suez Canal. The four-ship Skyhawk formations operated from medium altitude, and most reported scattered and ineffective AAA, while SAM launches were a rarity – a few were reported during Day 17, however. One No 110 Sqn Skyhawk suffered damage from an SA-3, but it landed safely at Refidim, in Sinai.

The missions against the 3rd Army were flown specifically to soften it up and prepare it for a siege after the ceasefire. In addition to conventional military targets, the Skyhawks also bombed water installations to worsen the conditions facing Egyptian troops during the siege. Large-scale CAS west of the Suez Canal helped ensure that IDF divisions had completed the encirclement of the 3rd Army by the time of the expected ceasefire. This did not happen, however, and it was probably why the ceasefire was not implemented during the evening hours of 22 October.

Skyhawk missions continued into the early hours of 23 October, when No 109 Sqn renewed operations over Mount Hermon following the observation of Syrian reinforcements. To frustrate a possible counterattack, No 109 Sqn Skyhawks flew 20 sorties against Syrian troop concentrations – 12 sorties in the morning and eight in the afternoon.

While No 109 Sqn flew over Mount Hermon, the other A-4 units prepared to resume air support operations over the Egyptian front. However, weather delayed take-offs until 0900 hrs. From then until sunset at 1702 hrs, the Skyhawks continuously bombed 3rd Army targets and supported IDF efforts to reach Ras Adabiya, and thus complete the encirclement of the enemy force. This Israeli objective was achieved by end of day, but the fighting still did not stop. Encirclement of the 3rd Army was complete, and it also included an enclave on the West Bank of the Suez Canal around Suez City. IDF troops had entered the latter, but urban warfare soon turned into a massive rescue mission as Israeli units became trapped within the Egyptian city. Thus, Skyhawk air support on 24 October focused on the Suez City sector, and was divided into two separate phases.

The first phase – normal CAS – commenced at 0549 hrs. Less than ten Skyhawk formations had taken off when there was news of another ceasefire deadline set for 0700 hrs. Further sorties were immediately called off. At 1030 hrs reports of fighting in Suez City as the IDF attempted to pull out reached the A-4 units, who launched jets to support this effort.

From noon, Skyhawk air strikes also covered the highway between Suez City and Cairo, along which armed clashes continued. Shortly before sunset at 1701 hrs, the final Skyhawk strike of the 'official' Yom Kippur War timeframe was launched over Suez City. The conflict was at last over, although Skyhawks continued to fly missions past the vague ceasefire hour that ended the war on 24 October 1973.

Perhaps the finest IDF/AF show of determination on a unit level during the Yom Kippur War was 102 Squadron's continued operations from Day 1 to Day 19. The squadron lost 17 Skyhawks, seven pilots were killed in action and five pilots became prisoners of war. In this image a 102 Squadron four-ship formation prepares for take-off from Hatzerim during the closing stages of the war. The leading pair are Crystal-equipped A-4Hs, tail numbers 11 and 25. The trailing pair are A-4Hs tail numbers 23 and 91; all four are loaded with five Rockeye cluster bomb units each. (via author)

COLOUR PLATES

1
A-4H BuNo 155242, Palmdale, California, 1967

2
A-4H IAF tail number 01, No 109 Sqn, Ramat David, 1968

3
A-4H IAF tail number 69, No 115 Sqn, Tel Nof, 1969

4
A-4E IAF tail number 208, No 116 Sqn, Tel Nof, 1971

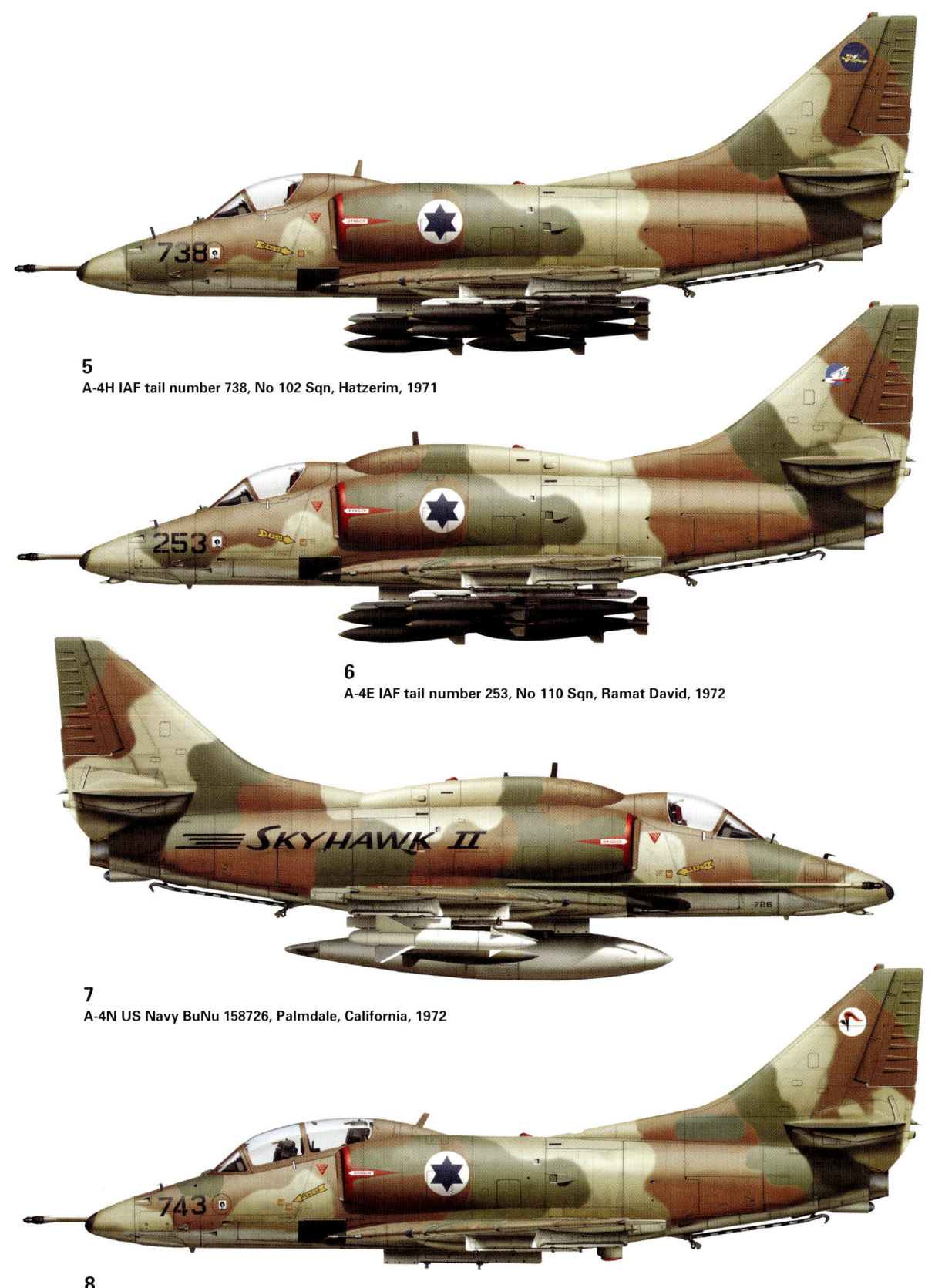

5
A-4H IAF tail number 738, No 102 Sqn, Hatzerim, 1971

6
A-4E IAF tail number 253, No 110 Sqn, Ramat David, 1972

7
A-4N US Navy BuNu 158726, Palmdale, California, 1972

8
TA-4H IAF tail number 743, Flying School Advanced Training Squadron, Hatzerim, 1972

9
A-4N IAF tail number 322, No 115 Sqn, Tel Nof, 1973

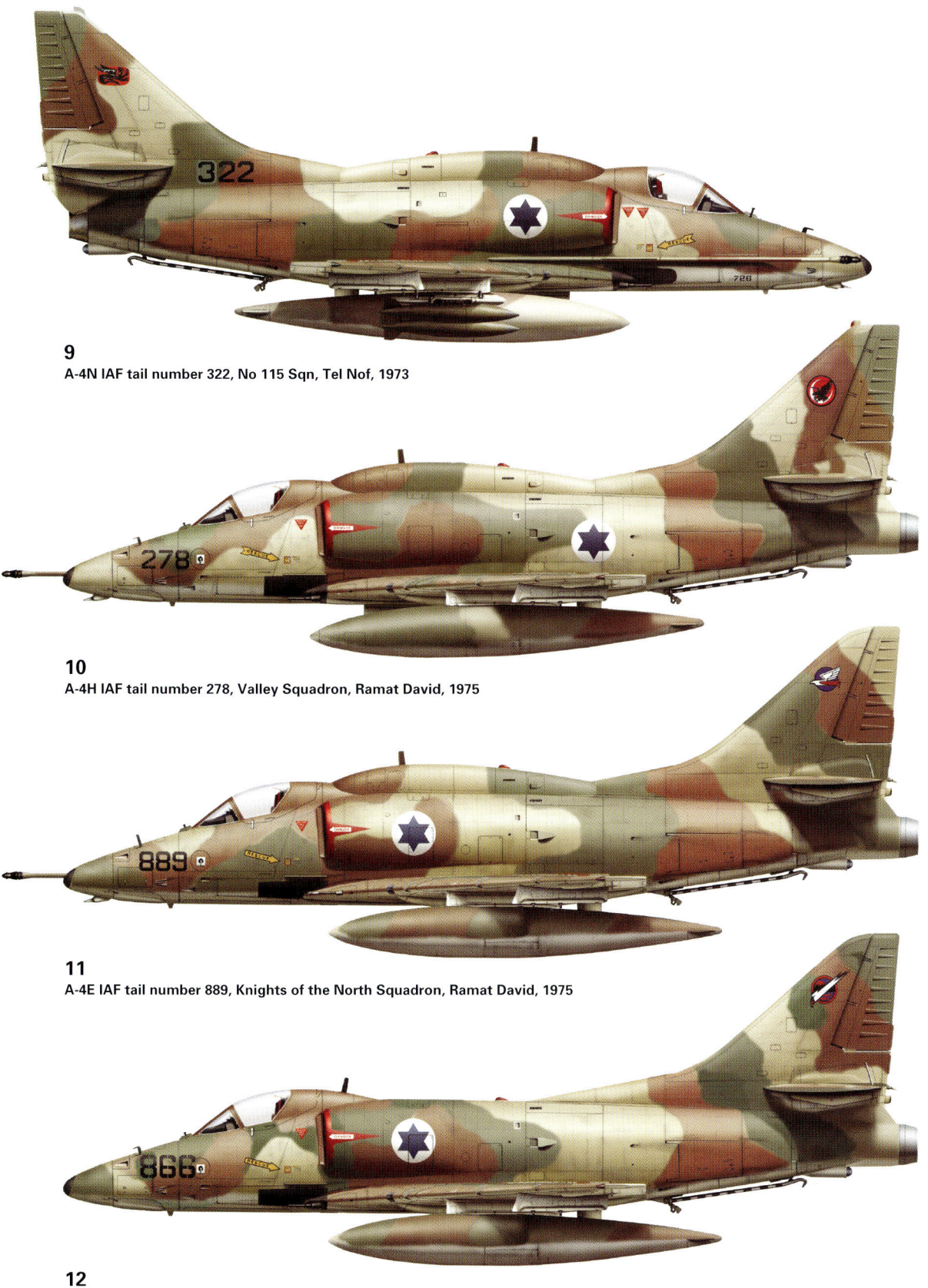

10
A-4H IAF tail number 278, Valley Squadron, Ramat David, 1975

11
A-4E IAF tail number 889, Knights of the North Squadron, Ramat David, 1975

12
A-4E IAF tail number 866, Shattering Parrot Squadron, Etszion, 1976

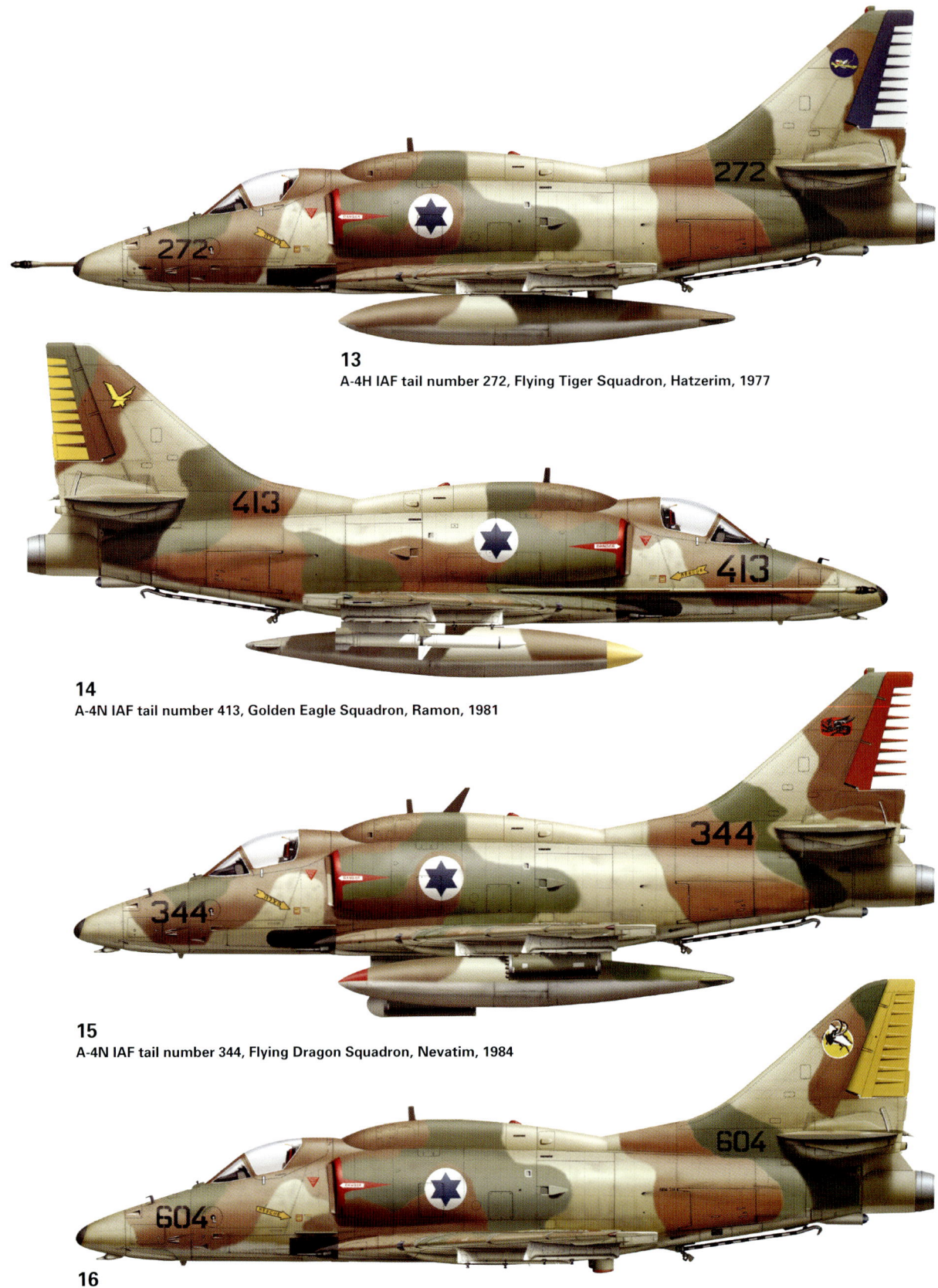

13
A-4H IAF tail number 272, Flying Tiger Squadron, Hatzerim, 1977

14
A-4N IAF tail number 413, Golden Eagle Squadron, Ramon, 1981

15
A-4N IAF tail number 344, Flying Dragon Squadron, Nevatim, 1984

16
A-4F IAF tail number 604, Flying Ibex Squadron, Hatzerim, 1986

17
A-4N IAF tail number 407, Flying Tiger Squadron, Hatzerim, 1986

18
A-4N IAF tail number 401, Flying Dragon Squadron, Nevatim, 1988

19
TA-4J IAF tail number 705, Flying School Advanced Training Squadron, Hatzerim, 1988

20
A-4N IAF tail number 328, Flying School Advanced Training Squadron/Flying Tiger Squadron, Hatzerim, 1992

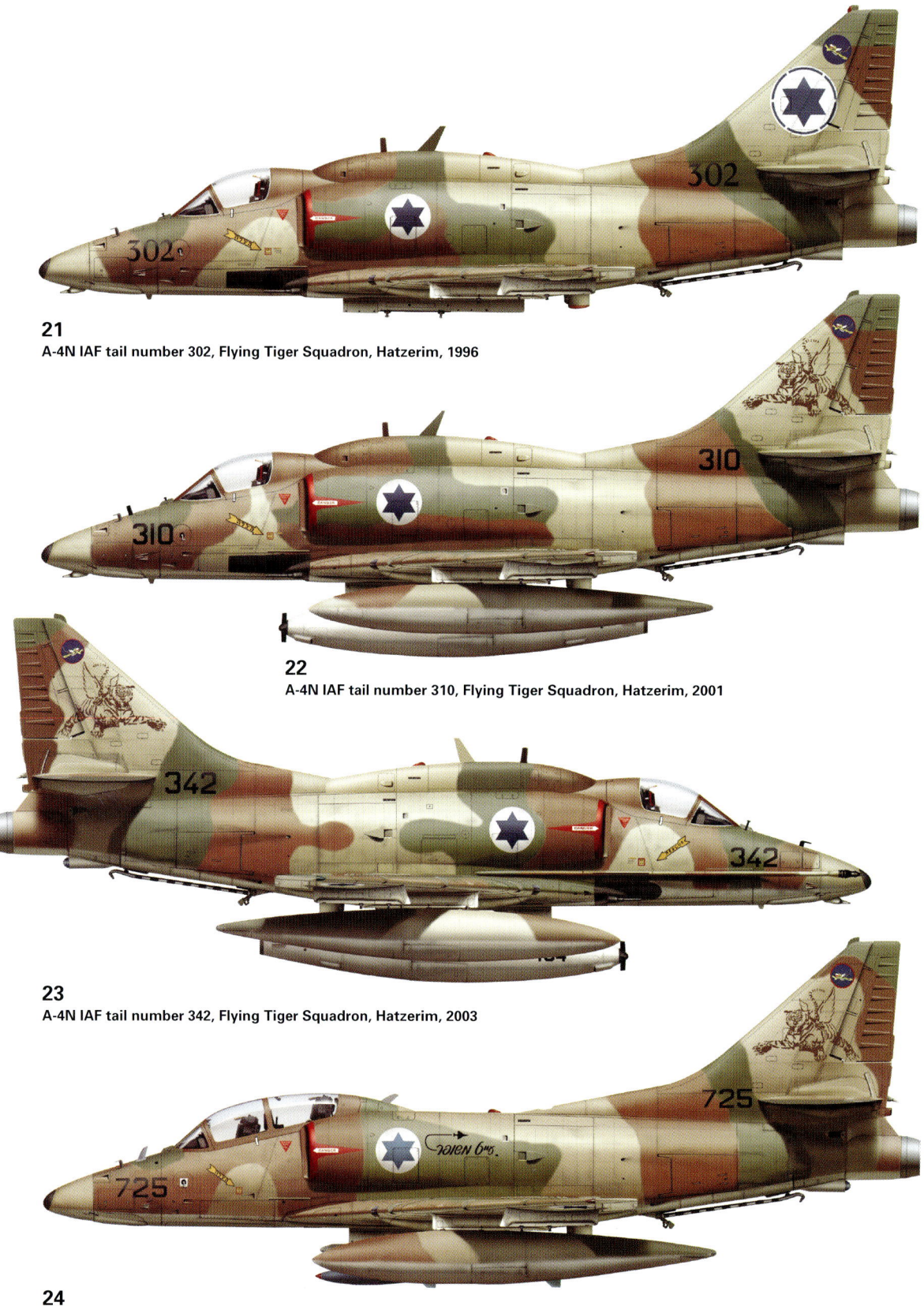

21
A-4N IAF tail number 302, Flying Tiger Squadron, Hatzerim, 1996

22
A-4N IAF tail number 310, Flying Tiger Squadron, Hatzerim, 2001

23
A-4N IAF tail number 342, Flying Tiger Squadron, Hatzerim, 2003

24
TA-4 IAF tail number 725, Flying Tiger Squadron, Hatzerim, 2007

1
No 109 Sqn

2
No 102 Sqn/Flying Tiger Squadron

3
No 115 Sqn

4
No 116 Sqn

5
No 110 Sqn

6
Golden Eagle Squadron

71

CHAPTER FOUR

SKYHAWK SUPREME

Yom Kippur War operations were the highlight of the Skyhawk's long history with the IDF/AF. The five operational squadrons had flown more than 4695 sorties over 19 days. These missions mostly covered close air support over two separate fronts against all manner of threats – AAA, SAMs and enemy fighters.

Many Israelis view the Yom Kippur War as a disaster, primarily because of the ratio between losses and gains when compared with the Six Day War. Without delving too much into that controversy, it is fair to compare the October 1973 Skyhawk force with the June 1967 Ouragan and Mystere force, since the Skyhawk was the direct light-attack aircraft replacement for the Ouragan and Mystere.

The statistics for the five Skyhawk squadrons during the Yom Kippur War make interesting reading. One squadron lost more aircraft than the others, another flew more sorties, a third squadron lost its commander and a fourth squadron entered the conflict with a CO who was not qualified to fly the Skyhawk operationally. The official IAF combat statistics for the five squadrons were as follows;

– No 102 Sqn flew 992 sorties and lost 17 aircraft for a loss rate of 1.7 percent

– No 109 Sqn flew 994 sorties and lost 13 aircraft for a loss rate of 1.3 percent

– No 110 Sqn flew 1136 sorties and lost 11 aircraft for a loss rate of 1 percent

– No 115 Sqn flew 750 sorties and lost seven aircraft for a loss rate of 0.9 percent

– No 116 Sqn flew 823 sorties and lost five aircraft for a loss rate of 0.6 percent

The combined loss rate (number of aircraft lost per 100 sorties) for the IAF Skyhawk force was 1.1 percent.

The IDF/AF's four Ouragan and Mystere squadrons flew 1374 sorties during the Six Day War and lost 17 aircraft for a loss rate of 1.2 percent. The Six Day War light attack aircraft generated an average of 229 sorties per day against an average of 247 sorties per day achieved by the Skyhawk squadrons during the Yom Kippur War. Average number of losses was 2.8 light attack aircraft per day in both wars!

The effect of air superiority on combat attrition was obviously significant. The popular narratives usually state that the Six Day War air superiority battle lasted one day and yielded five fighting days with total Israeli air supremacy. This was not the case, however, for IDF/AF air superiority missions, including air base attacks and SEAD, continued past Day 1. Therefore, the fact that IDF/AF had to extend the air superiority campaign during the Yom Kippur War should not have come as a surprise to anyone with even the slightest knowledge of Six Day War operations.

Most air superority missions in the Six Day War were flown on Day 1, or for a timeframe of 18 percent of the war. This correlates to more than three days in the Yom Kippur War, or from Days 1 to 4. Light-attack aircraft losses during these periods were nine Ouragans and Mysteres in the Six Day War and 31 Skyhawks in the Yom Kippur War. The critical initial phase of both conflicts cost the IDF/AF 53 percent and 58 percent of total light-attack aircraft losses in the Six Day War and Yom Kippur War, respectively.

The IDF/AF Skyhawk force continued to expand and modernise following the Yom Kippur War. The 'Barrel' modification was incorporated into the modernisation process, additional A-4Ns arrived, Yom Kippur War emergency aid jets had to be modified to Israeli standards and the force structure was adapted to suit lessons learned in the conflict.

Yom Kippur War losses and emergency aid both depleted the A-4H fleet and augmented stocks of the A-4E/F. Adjustments had to be made because of this imbalance, including the Flying Tiger Squadron (formerly No 102 Sqn) adding A-4Es to its original inventory of A-4Hs. In line with pre-Yom Kippur War plans, the Flying Wing Squadron (formerly No 116 Sqn) resumed conversion to the A-4N and the Golden Eagle Squadron's activation process as an A-4E unit at Etszion was renewed. Its OTU Course 1 started in November 1973, and a new course commenced each April, August and November until 1985.

Restructuring the Skyhawk force during the months that followed the Yom Kippur War ran parallel with ongoing combat operations. At first, the Syrian frontier was quiet, while armed clashes continued in the south beyond the ceasefire H-Hour. The largest of these occurred on 26 October 1973 when Skyhawks flew nearly 100 sorties against 3rd Army targets including bridges over the Suez Canal that connected the besieged force east of the waterway with the Egyptian enclave in Suez City on the west side of the canal.

Up north, hostilities resumed in the spring of 1974 as snow melted to expose the barren summit of Mount Hermon. Flying CAS over the mountainous terrain of the Mount Hermon sector was hazardous, but essential. The A-4s started operations on 6 April, attacking troop concentrations, armoured vehicles and heavy engineering equipment that was being used by the Syrians to build roads to the summit. A new Skyhawk mission introduced over Mount Hermon at this time saw jets dispensing chaff screens. Another milestone was the first operational mission flown by the new Golden Eagle Squadron, which sent a four-ship formation of jets into combat on 14 April.

Valley Squadron A-4H Skyhawk tail number 229 at Ramat David, ready for a mission against Syria in April 1974. The Skyhawk is in a somewhat unorthodox configuration with five general purpose bombs loaded one to each of the five weapon stations in what the IDF/AF called 'direct slinging'. From the late stages of the Yom Kippur War, the mixed two- and three-digit tail number system was streamlined into three-digit tail numbers with the first digit indicating batch, configuration or model. Surviving A-4H Skyhawks that pre-war had a two-digit tail number (with prefix '1' added to Valley Squadron aircraft and prefix '7' added to Flying Tiger Squadron aircraft) were thus standardized with three-digit tail numbers prefixed by '2', so that pre-war Valley Squadron's A-4H tail number 129 became Skyhawk 229. (via author)

CHAPTER FOUR

The scale and intensity of the air strikes escalated to a peak on 19 April, when IDF/AF combat aircraft flew 308 sorties. A pair of Knights of the North Squadron (formerly No 110 Sqn) Skyhawks attacking Syrian outposts were warned of incoming SAMs immediately after dropping their ordnance. The wingman's jet then crashed, killing Aryeh Dobnov.

From early May 1974 the IDF/AF extended its combat theatre to cover 'Fatahland', a district in Lebanon west of Mount Hermon that the PLO used as a base for operations against Israel. By the end of May 1974, Israel and Syria had finally agreed to a ceasefire, but IDF/AF operations continued over Lebanon.

Skyhawk strikes against Palestinian targets in Lebanon became almost routine from May 1974. The Palestinians had no proper air defence assets except for improvised AAA and shoulder-launched SAMs. The latter undoubtedly posed the greater threat, but the 'Barrel' modification soon proved its effectiveness. Occasionally, SA-7s did indeed hit Skyhawks, but thanks to 'Barrel', battle damage was never severe. From 20 June 1974, Skyhawks with damaged tail sections usually diverted, or returned for an emergency landing at Ramat David. The first jet to do this was a Flying Wing Squadron A-4 on an AGM-62 Walleye attack mission over Burj El Shemali refugee camp east of Tyre.

Ongoing deliveries of A-4Ns meant that the Valley Squadron equipped with A-4Hs from May 1974 and the Golden Eagle Squadron converted from the A-4E to the N-model in May 1976. Many of the redundant Golden Eagle Squadron A-4Es remained at Etszion air base, where they were assigned to the Shattering Parrot Squadron that was activated in July 1976 as the eighth Israeli Skyhawk unit.

This peak force strength for the A-4 was achieved well after the Skyhawk's successor had entered frontline service, and parallel with Israeli acquisition negotiations for an even more advanced replacement. The former was the indigenous Israel Aircraft Industries Kfir (which, in many ways, was a faster Skyhawk), the first of which reached the frontline in 1975. The latter was the General Dynamics F-16 Fighting Falcon that would enter IDF/AF service in 1980, initially more as a replacement for the Mirage III and Nesher rather than the Skyhawk.

A-4N deliveries and the standard upgrade of earlier models began to wind down in 1976. Indeed, the Skyhawk replacement process commenced only a year after peak strength had been achieved when the

Northern Knights Squadron's A-4E Skyhawk tail number 862 returns from a mission to its hardened aircraft shelter at Ramat David air base. Skyhawk 862 was a pre-Yom Kippur War A-4E delivery originally flown as Skyhawk 262; the paintwork that transformed 262 into 862 is clearly visible as is IDF/AF-style air-intake warning titles. Yom Kippur War emergency aid A-4E Skyhawks were also assigned prefix '8' tail numbers and were initially distinguished because of US Navy-style air-intake warnings that were taped over during the hasty repainting process. (via author)

Valley Squadron traded its jets for Kfirs in July 1977. However, the the IDF/AF's Skyhawk replacement programme has yet to be completed, for examples of the jet remain in service more than 30 years later.

OPERATION *LITANI*

Palestinian attacks on Israel from Lebanon lessened after the civil war erupted in the latter country during April 1975. But they increased once again after Syria invaded Lebanon in the spring of 1976. The final Skyhawk air strike during this round of fighting came on 2 December 1975 when 32 jets were assigned to attack PLO targets at Nar El Bard, near Tripoli in northern Lebanon, and in the Nabatiya sector in the south of the country.

Air strikes recommenced in the autumn of 1977 when Skyhawks returned to Lebanese skies on 9 November to bomb PLO targets in reprisal for rocket attacks against the Israeli city of Nahariya. Hostilities escalated until Israel launched Operation *Litani* on 15 March 1978. Its primary objective was to occupy southern Lebanon up to the Litani River, and mop up the infrastructure supporting Palestinian armed groups in this area.

Operation *Litani* saw the largest incursion of Israeli troops into Lebanon up to that point, but it was too confined in terms of available targets, territory and timescale for the commencement of full-scale operations involving all six frontline Skyhawk squadrons.

The Skyhawks primarily flew three types of missions – air strikes against targets well defined in operational orders, CAS with real-time target assignments through an air liaison officer and nighttime illumination. The number of Palestinian targets in southern Lebanon was small, so there was little planned air strike activity, and there were far more Skyhawks available than were required for the small number of CAS calls made in support of ground forces. Illustrating the scale of operations during *Litani*, the Flying Wing Squadron flew just 29 sorties (including one nighttime illumination) and the Golden Eagle Squadron completed 19 sorties (including two nighttime illuminations).

Palestinian opposition to this excessive demonstration of Israeli air power was minimal – a shoulder-launched SAM damaged the lead aircraft of a Flying Wing Squadron four-ship formation on an air strike mission over the Damur sector. The Skyhawk's ability to survive such attacks had vastly improved by now, and the pilot landed safely at Ramat David.

Five months after *Litani*, the Skyhawk force again fielded eight squadrons. The new unit was the Flying Ibex Squadron. Based at Hatzerim, it was supposed to be manned in the main by reserve pilots, along with a cadre of IDF/AF regulars. However, this force split was not favoured by either reservists or regulars, and it was dropped prior to activation of the Flying Ibex Squadron in August 1978 as a standard IDF/AF light strike unit with the usual composition of regulars, emergency postings and reserves.

Ramat David was the northernmost IDF/AF fighter base and was thus an ideal recovery field for damaged aircraft returning from missions over Lebanon or Syria. Two Tel Nof-based Flying Wing Squadron's battle-damaged A-4N Skyhawks landed at Ramat David in May and June 1974. The May 1974 landing involved a Skyhawk damaged over Syria and in the illustrated 20 June 1974 incident, A-4N tail number 354 returned from a mission over Lebanon with substantial battle damage from an SA-7 hit. (via author)

CHAPTER FOUR

Litani changed the political situation in south Lebanon, for Israel began sponsoring the South Lebanon Army that occupied a security zone along a strip of land north of the Israeli-Lebanese border. This zone calmed the theatre down for a short while, but hostilities eventually escalated once again. The A-4s returned to attack PLO targets in December 1978, and from April 1979 the tempo of air strikes accelerated.

The Flying Ibex Squadron flew its first operational mission on 24 April 1979 when it attacked Palestinian artillery north of Tyre. By then the nature of warfare had changed because of the security zone, with Palestinian attacks mostly involving artillery fire and rockets. Many Skyhawk missions over Lebanon, therefore, targeted artillery pieces and rocket launchers. The PLO would camouflage and hide their weapons, so this mission became increasingly difficult to perform. A lack of precision-guided munitions reduced Skyhawk effectiveness in such surgical operations too. Although somewhat discouraged, Skyhawk pilots resorted to flying strafing passes during the 1979 campaign against PLO artillery and rockets in Lebanon chiefly because bombing rarely achieved the desired results.

Israeli and Syrian intervention in the Lebanese Civil War, coupled with the signing of the peace treaty between Egypt and Israel, resulted in intensified action over Lebanon. Syrian interceptors started flying over the country in an effort to protect their Palestinian allies from Israeli air strikes, thus providing a new threat for Skyhawk pilots to be wary of. Although they did not directly engage Syrian fighters over Lebanon, Skyhawk air strikes occasionally triggered air combat when Syrian jets were vectored to intercept attack aircraft and Israeli CAPs were sent to defend them.

Such was the scenario on 27 June 1979 when two pairs of Flying Tiger Squadron Skyhawks took part in air strikes over the Sidon sector that eventually provoked the first major air combat between Israeli and Syrian fighters over Lebanon during the Lebanese Civil War.

LASER-GUIDED BOMBS

The Skyhawk's principal precision-guided munition in Israeli service during the 1970s was the AGM-62 Walleye TV-guided glide bomb. The Walleye was not well-suited to counter-terrorist operations of the type the IAF experienced over Lebanon, however. In fact the AGM-62 was probably more expensive than most of the Palestinian targets the IDF/AF attacked! TV guidance limited delivery to good weather, and above

The post-Yom Kippur War restructuring of the tail number system issued three prefix digits to TA-4 two-seat Skyhawks: prefix '1' was assigned to TA-4F, prefix '5' identified TA-4H and prefix '7' TA-4J trainers. Skyhawk 164 was photographed in December 1975 when serving the Golden Eagle Squadron at Etszion; the new squadron badge was painted on Golden Eagle Squadron Skyhawks from December 1973. (via author)

Skyhawk squadrons started to introduce colourful rudder artwork from 1976. The initial artwork took advantage of the Skyhawk's rudder surface with roughly half rudder width stripes painted over the principal colour. The first three styles of rudder artwork to appear were the Flying Wing Squadron's pattern of red with white stripes, the Flying Tiger Squadron's version of blue with white stripes, and the Golden Eagle Squadron's yellow with green stripes. Flying Wing Squadron's A-4N Skyhawk tail number 308 was photographed in May 1976 at Etszion already adorned with the characteristic rudder: red with white stripes. (via author)

The pre-Yom Kippur War homogenous inventory of Flying Tiger Squadron's A-4H inventory was considerably depleted so post-war, the squadron flew a mix of three single-seat versions: A-4E with prefix '8', A-4F with prefix '6', and A-4H with prefix '2'. Regardless of origin, all three IAF types of early Skyhawks were upgraded to a similar standard with 30 mm cannon, Crystal and higher-rated engines as principal components. A-4F Skyhawk tail number 612 was photographed taxiing at Hatzerim in July 1977 adorned with the Flying Wing Squadron's rudder artwork of blue with white stripes. (via author)

Tel Nof hosted the IDF/AF Skyhawk force day in June 1978. The line included, from left to right: Shattering Parrot Squadron's A-4N tail number 343, Northern Knights Squadron's A-4H tail number 229, Golden Eagle Squadron's A-4N tail number 306, Flying Tiger Squadron's A-4H tail number 235, and Flying Wing Squadron's A-4N tail number 392. The IDF/AF activated seven Skyhawk squadrons prior to the Yom Kippur War and added two more Skyhawk squadrons in 1976 and 1978, thus creating the largest IDF/AF fighter force community until the introduction of the F-16 Fighting Falcon from 1980, though naturally it took a while until the Fighting Falcon caught up with the Skyhawk. (via author)

average skills were imperative for best results. A less expensive, less complicated and less demanding precision-guided weapon duly replaced it as the IDF/AF's standard guided munition in counter-terrorist attacks over Lebanon. It was the laser-guided bomb (LGB).

The Flying Wing Squadron joined the initial cadre of IDF/AF LGB capable squadrons in 1980. The LGB qualification did not include 'lasing', however – designating a target with a laser beam. Skyhawk pilots relied on target designation from other laser-capable combat aircraft, attack helicopters, unmanned aerial vehicles or a ground-based IDF elite unit lasing team. Supporting the Flying Wing Squadron laser-guided bomb qualification was the AN/AAS-35 Pave Penny laser spot tracking pod.

The peak number of eight Skyhawk squadrons was not maintained for long. The world media reported in 1979 the possible export of surplus Israeli A-4s to Malaysia, but this sale did not materialise. A deal that did go through, however, was the export of 16 Skyhawks to Indonesia, which the US government officially admitted in October 1979. Meanwhile, Kfir deliveries accelerated and F-16s arrived from July 1980. Shortly afterwards, the Knights of the North Squadron converted to the F-16 and the Shattering Parrot Squadron became a Kfir unit.

Redeployment of the surviving Skyhawk squadrons was also planned, as Israel had to return Sinai to Egyptian control by April 1982 in line with terms of the Egyptian-Israeli peace treaty. The IDF/AF had two major air bases in Sinai plus numerous other airfields, installations and sites. US compensation covered the construction of two new air bases in the Negev Desert – a project that was started in 1979 with Ramon and Ovda air bases in the Negev replacing Eitham and Etszion in Sinai.

CHAPTER FOUR

Israel commenced construction of a third new air base in the Negev, Nevatim. The IDF/AF redeployment plan covered half of the frontline Skyhawk force, with the Golden Eagle Squadron planned to move out of Etszion and into Ramon. Later still, the Tel Nof squadrons, Flying Dragon and Flying Wing Squadrons, would occupy Nevatim.

The intensity of IDF/AF offensive operations over Lebanon was usually linked to the level of friction between the four principal players – Israel, the Lebanese Christian militia, the Palestinians and Syria. There was little activity between July 1979 and July 1980, when no Skyhawk missions were reported. The A-4s returned to attack PLO targets from 20 August 1980, although strikes were again sporadic – attacks were made on 7 November 1980, 31 December 1980, 29 January 1981 and 2 March 1981. The Skyhawks operated mostly over south Lebanon, and occasionally SyAAF fighters were scrambled to defend the Palestinians.

A few air strikes triggered aerial engagements, including the 31 December 1980 bombings in the Nabatiya sector. A shoulder-launched SAM damaged a Skyhawk on 29 January 1981, but the 'Barrel' modification again proved its worth and the Skyhawk pilot made an emergency landing at Ramat David.

Israeli air strikes in Lebanon intensified from April 1981. By then, Israel had forged an alliance with the Lebanese Christian militia. Syria launched an offensive against the latter in the Zahle sector that same month, and Israel felt obliged to support its allies. The Palestinians lent a hand to their then-patron in Lebanon, Syria. Skyhawk air strikes in this round of intensified operations started on 9 April. The IDF launched a major assault against Palestinian targets in the Arab El Salim sector during the night of 9/10 April, and five IDF/AF squadrons took part in the preparatory air strikes, including the Tel Nof Skyhawk units.

Seven years after the Yom Kippur War, and despite continuous low-intensity operations over Lebanon, many of the Skyhawk pilots now lacked operational experience. Three of the four pilots in a Flying Wing Squadron four-ship formation flew their first-ever operational mission during an air strike against the Palestinian maritime unit base at Ras El Ain, south of Rashidiya, on 16 April. The Skyhawks participated in four more air raids from 20 to 29 April.

On 28 April, IDF/AF jets had shot down two Syrian helicopters supporting troops in their offensive against the Lebanese Christian militia in the Zahle sector. In reprisal, the Syrians inserted a network of SAM batteries in the Lebanon Valley. The Israeli government took a dim view of this action and ordered the IDF/AF to prepare for SEAD missions in order to destroy the SAM batteries. However, at that time the IDF/AF was also preparing for another higher-priority operation, so the air offensive against the SAMs in the Lebanon Valley was put on hold.

The 'other operation' was a long-range air strike against Iraq's uncompleted Osirak nuclear reactor that was launched on 7 June 1981. Obviously, Skyhawks did not take

The Flying Ibex Squadron was activated in August 1978 with a mix of A-4E, A-4F and A-4N Skyhawks. The Initial Operational Capability (IOC) milestone was achieved on 1 April 1979 and the squadron's operational debut was on 24 April 1979, when a four-ship formation attacked Palestinian artillery north of Tyre. A-4N tail number 377 was photographed at Hatzerim prior to departure on this mission, armed with a 'conventional' IDF/AF Skyhawk warload of that era: six 500-lb Mk 82 bombs attached to the MER under the fuselage and two more Mk 82 bombs under the outer wing stations, for a total offensive load of nearly 2,000 kg. (via author)

The short range from Ramat David to targets in southern Lebanon enabled the Skyhawk squadrons to dispense with external fuel tanks and to lift a maximum offensive external load on 'routine security' missions against Palestinian targets in Lebanon. The Northern Knights Squadron's A-4H Skyhawk tail number 241 was photographed on 20 August 1980 before a mission over Lebanon loaded with ten 500-lb Mk 82 bombs: six attached to a MER under the fuselage and four in 'direct slinging' under the wing stations. (via author)

part in this operation, although the Golden Eagle Squadron hosted the Operation *Opera* strike force prior to its departure to Iraq from Etszion.

Skyhawk air strikes in Lebanon were mostly aimed at targets in the southern part of the country, with occasional attacks against targets farther north, but still south of the Beirut-Damascus highway. A deeper incursion came on 28 May when Skyhawks bombed targets in the Lebanon Valley, possibly to 'tease and test' the recently installed Syrian SAMs.

In June the IDF/AF level of offensive operations in the Lebanese theatre was reduced, but in July things almost got out of hand. The IDF clashed with the PLO, the latter shelling and rocketing Israeli cities, towns and villages, while the IDF/AF unleashed its air power in a series of massive air strikes all over southern Lebanon. Skyhawks participated in the offensive from 12 to 23 July, bombing targets that included civil infrastructure (bridges and roads), military infrastructure (barracks, bunkers, headquarters and outposts) and weapons (AAA, artillery pieces, rocket launchers, tanks and vehicles). Again, most Skyhawk missions were over the south, with the exception of a 17 July operation that saw A-4s taking part in major IDF/AF air strike against the Palestinian headquarters in Beirut.

The July 1981 escalation ended in another ceasefire between Israel and the Palestinians, which was welcomed primarily because the IDF/AF was busy implementing the Sinai evacuation redeployment plan. The Golden Eagle Squadron moved from Etszion to Ramon in November 1981. To speed up this process, the Flying Wing Squadron lent a hand with the OTU course from August 1981.

Israel completed the evacuation of Sinai in April 1982, leaving the IDF/AF to deal with the threat in the north. Air strikes over Lebanon resumed on 21 April when massive bombings targeted a PLO training camp south of Damur. Skyhawks took part in the mission that destroyed the camp, killing 20 Palestinians and injuring 60 more. Syrian fighters were sent to intercept the attacking aircraft, and the IDF/AF claimed two Syrian MiG-23s shot down. The situation in Lebanon was now on a knife edge, and major escalation was expected. IDF units were placed on alert in readiness for Operation *Pines* – another Israeli invasion of Lebanese territory.

There were several versions of *Pines*, sometimes referred to as *Small Pines* and *Big Pines*, depending on scale and objectives. The basic idea was to push the Palestinians north of the Israeli-Lebanese border to a line beyond the range of their artillery and rockets. The larger-scale *Pines* plan added the expulsion of Palestinian armed groups from Lebanon, the link-up with the Lebanese Christian militia and the destruction of the Syrian air defense force deployment in the Lebanon Valley. The IDF was ready to activate *Pines* from April 1982 as Israel waited for a catalyst.

This came in the form of an assassination attempt that critically wounded the Israeli ambassador in London on 3 June 1982. Israel

CHAPTER FOUR

pointed a finger at the Palestinians and ordered the IAF to launch massive air strikes against nine targets in Lebanon. H-Hour was 1515 hrs on Friday, 4 June 1982. Predictably, the Palestinians returned fire, shelling and rocketing Israel from 1645 hrs.

A Flying Dragon Squadron four-ship formation was scrambled at 1645 hrs, and it attacked a Palestinian 130 mm artillery piece north of Nabatiya. Soon, it became apparent that the Palestinians had also used the previous year to build up their flak installations. AAA fire was extensive, and at 1725 hrs a Flying Dragon Squadron section took off to attack an AAA site near the estuary of the Zahrani River. Three of the six Flying Dragon Squadron pilots flying operational sorties on 4 June were performing their first combat mission. From sunset at 1840 hrs till dawn at 0438 hrs, IDF/AF attack helicopters roamed over southern Lebanon attacking 22 Palestinian targets. There was a full moon, but the attack helicopter crews had only limited nocturnal capabilities, so throughout the night Skyhawks illuminated the sky for their benefit.

Four Flying Wing Squadron A-4N Skyhawks line up at Tel Nof prior to an attack mission over Lebanon during the hot summer of 1981. A-4N tail numbers 376, 392, 332 and 356 are loaded with ten 500-lb Mk 82 bombs each. At the time, the bulk of the Skyhawk force was used primarily as ballistic bombers, using a lot of general purpose unguided bombs to attack small targets on the ground for 'statistical kills' on probability that 'X' percent of the 'Y' weapons dropped would hit the target. By then, however, the concept of expending fewer, more precise weapons was gaining hold among other IDF/AF fighter force communities – notably the Phantom force – but the Skyhawk force somewhat lagged behind in precision-guidance munitions. (via author)

Flying Dragon Squadron A-4N Skyhawk tail number 327 was photographed in August 1981 after returning from a mission over Lebanon with damage from an SA-7. The illustrated damage clearly highlights the benefits of the Yom Kippur War-era 'Barrel' modification that extended the Skyhawk's nozzle specifically to combat the SA-7 threat. The missile's warhead explosion extensively damaged the 'Barrel' but inflicted little damage to the original jet pipe. (via author)

The first phase of IDF/AF redeployment in the wake of the March 1979 peace treaty between Egypt and Israel was accomplished in November 1981 when the Golden Eagle Squadron moved from Etszion air base in Sinai to the new US-built Ramon air base in the Negev. At the time the Golden Eagle Squadron was responsible for the IDF/AF's fighter OTU course and was the largest IDF/AF fighter squadron. The Golden Eagle Squadron flew a mix of more than 40 A-4E, A-4N and TA-4 Skyhawks including A-4E tail number 899 that was photographed at Etszion prior to final departure on the ferry flight to Ramon in November 1981. (via author)

The exchange of artillery shelling, rocket attacks and air strikes escalated during Saturday, 5 June. IDF/AF attack aircraft, including Skyhawks, hammered Palestinian targets in southern Lebanon. The use of Israeli air power was excessive, as there were few legitimate Palestinian targets remaining by this stage in the campaign. On many missions Skyhawk pilots flew racetrack patterns for a considerable time before making their attacks, primarily because southern Lebanese air space was full of Israeli aircraft. Most weapons were still not precision-guided, so on many occasions targets were erroneously reported as destroyed.

A example was the 130 mm artillery piece north of Nabatiya that the Flying Dragon Squadron attacked on the afternoon of 4 June. Reported destroyed, that same cannon was active the very next day, so another Flying Dragon Squadron four-ship formation (a unit that already knew the target well) departed Tel Nof at 1205 hrs to bomb the surviving artillery piece, and the formation also reported its destruction.

Rocket attacks were also flown with four to six rocket pods. All were launched in a single salvo from medium altitude in a dive to avoid jeopardising survivability. Pilots felt as though the aircraft literally stopped in the air when launching so many rockets at once. Yet their effectiveness was again dubious. A Golden Eagle Squadron pair tasked to attack an artillery piece hidden in a small forest west of Nabatiya duly struck the exact location as required. However, when their films were analysed, the artillery piece was noted as still being intact inside a trench several hundred metres away from the aiming point.

By evening, it became apparent that IDF/AF aircraft and IDF artillery were unable to suppress Palestinian artillery shelling and rocket attacks. This could hardly have surprised anyone with knowledge of Attrition War operations and previous Israeli campaigns against the Palestinians in Lebanon. In fact, Israel's mighty air power is still striving to achieve such an objective. Air strikes continued past sunset at 1841 hrs nonetheless. While aircraft, including Skyhawks, were bombing targets in Lebanon, the Israeli government ordered the IDF to mobilise for invasion. This plan was announced to the world as Operation *Peace for Galilee*. The 'advertised' objective was to stop Palestinian shelling and rocketing of Israel's northern district.

D-Day for the invasion was Sunday, 6 June 1982, and H-Hour was 1100 hrs. Prior to this, air strikes continued. The Flying Dragon Squadron launched two four-ship formations, both tasked with attacking targets in the Nabatiya sector. The first formation attacked as planned and returned safely to Tel Nof. The second formation that departed at 0740 hrs reported losing its No 3. The Skyhawk was seen to explode in mid-air near the ruins of the ancient Beaufort fortress. Israeli sources initially attributed the loss to some sort of anti-aircraft fire. Syrian sources stated that an El Saika (a Palestinian faction created and controlled by Syria) SA-7 team was positioned in the Beaufort fortress, and that it had shot down the Skyhawk. With hindsight, the SA-7 option was the probable cause of this loss. Reserve pilot Aharon Achiaz ejected and was held prisoner by the Palestinians until released on 20 August 1982.

Targets bombed during the hours that preceded invasion included artillery, fortifications and roads. Additionally, the Skyhawks flew leaflet drop missions, their 'cargo' addressing Lebanese citizens in effort to explain the Israeli invasion. Once IDF units crossed the border, CAS was added to the Skyhawk portfolio of missions, as well as smoke screening to disrupt the observation of IDF movements.

The invasion spearhead had reached the Litani River by the end of Day 1. The next morning, IDF troops started to mop up the city of Tyre, which was home to many armed Palestinians. Skyhawks supported this action from 0700 hrs when they dropped leaflets over the city, urging citizens to concentrate at the beach. The IDF reported that 12,000 citizens answered the leaflet's call and headed for the coast, but many more remained in their homes, caught up in the ruthless urban warfare in the city and surrounding refugee camps, which lasted four days.

A few Day 2 Skyhawk missions ranged deeper into Lebanon, including a Flying Dragon Squadron four-ship formation that raided a Palestinian headquarters compound near Damur at noon. Each of the jets was carrying six rocket pods that were fired in two passes.

Aerial leaflet drops were flown on the night of 7/8 June over Sidon. The civil population was again asked to concentrate at the beach in preparation for the IDF campaign to clear the city of armed Palestinians that began in the early morning hours of Day 3 and was only completed on 15 June. While IDF infantry brigades were involved in urban fighting at Tyre and Sidon, the armoured brigades pressed north towards Beirut in the west and the Beirut-Damascus highway in the east.

During the day, Israeli and Syrians forces exchanged fire as IDF units came closer to the southern limits of the engagement envelope of the Syrian air defence force deployed in the Lebanon Valley. As usual, air superiority was essential to ensure unrestricted air support. The IAF was ordered to prepare for the activation of Operation *Mole Cricket 19*.

Golden Eagle Squadron A-4N Skyhawk tail number 405 catching a cable on a Ramon runway sometime after the Lebanon War. The Golden Eagle Squadron experienced several take-off tyre-shredding peel incidents during the June 1982 Lebanon War. This phenomenon was not experienced during peacetime operations and was attributed to higher gross weights during wartime coupled with a slightly upward-sloping runway, the relatively high-altitude location of Ramon, and high summer temperatures that affected both aircraft performance and the interaction between black runways and black tyres, which all became very hot. Luckily for the Golden Eagle Squadron, none of the June 1982 Lebanon War tyre incidents escalated into an accident. Interestingly, the Ramon wartime tyre issue resurfaced during the July to August 2006 Lebanon War and this time, one of the incidents caused a major accident that resulted in the pilot ejecting on the runway (via author)

Its objective was the destruction of the Syrian air defence force in the Lebanon Valley. The operation's numbering indicated 19 surface-to-air missile batteries that were all to be attacked.

Day 3 air support activity was lower than usual as Skyhawk squadrons received orders to prepare for *Mole Cricket 19*. Simultaneously, a small-scale preparatory operation was launched to suppress and destroy Syrian radar stations south of Beirut. This was accomplished in two waves from 1330 hrs, with attack helicopters in the first wave, immediately followed by Skyhawks.

Personnel involved in *Mole Cricket 19* were briefed that evening, but approval for the operation was not given until 8 June 1982. Instead, air strikes were intensified during the afternoon hours, but the concentration of so many attack aircraft over a rather small sector in the eastern frontline where the Israeli and Syrian forces clashed resulted in many mid-air changes as formations orbited and waited for their turn to attack.

A typical example was a Flying Dragon Squadron formation tasked to bomb Syrian tanks with Rockeye anti-armour CBUs at dusk. This target was changed to mortars en route to the attack sector. Communication jamming was experienced when the formation contacted the air liaison officer and clouds prevented positive identification of the target. Distant SAM launches painted white trails amid the dusk sky. Unable to receive alternative targets due to communication jamming and the approaching sunset, the Skyhawk pilots joined up with a neighbouring formation and attacked its target instead.

IDF armoured columns raced north from Day 1 to Day 3, well past the 40-km point north of the Israeli-Lebanese border that was considered to be sufficiently far enough away from Israel to keep it safe from Palestinian artillery and rocket attacks. The Israeli military objective was now the Beirut-Damascus highway. Syrian troops were deployed in Beirut, along the highway and south of it too, mostly in the east. The engagement envelope of the Syrian air defence deployment in the Lebanon Valley defended units that clashed with IDF forces on 8 June. Air superiority was indeed crucial for effective air support, but internal controversy surrounded the launch of Operation *Mole Cricket 19*.

Protagonists claimed that air superiority was essential for effective CAS, and they hoped for a new campaign that would erase the memory of the October 1973 Yom Kippur War Operations *Challenge 4* and *Model 5*. Opponents argued that IDF/AF preparations since 1973 for an air superiority battle against SAMs should be reserved for major war, and not wasted for the benefit of a limited scale operation such as this.

Misgivings lasted more than 24 hours, by which point Syrian forces had been involved in hostilities since 8 June. The IDF/AF finally got the order to proceed at noon the next day. The activation order was distributed to squadrons while Skyhawks were busy attacking ground targets, mostly in the Damur

The air warfare highlight of the June 1982 Lebanon War was IDF/AF Operation *Mole Cricket 19* aimed at destroying Syrian air defences in the Lebanon Valley. The Skyhawks were not in the thick of the air superiority battle and mostly flew peripheral support missions including chaff laying, launching decoys, and anti-radiation missile patrols. The Skyhawk's anti-radiation missile was the old AGM-45 Shrike that, like its carrying platform, was secondary to air- and ground-launched versions of the AGM-78 Standard ARM. (via author)

CHAPTER FOUR

The Skyhawk's principal mission in Israeli service was air support but during the Lebanon War, the IDF/AF simply had an excess of air power for the task. The Lebanon theatre was limited in size and there were not enough targets to fully employ all the IDF/AF's assets. New warplanes, that in a full-scale war would have been busy in 'higher value' missions, were assigned to fly air support and the Skyhawks' slice of overall operations was cut accordingly. As illustrated, the Skyhawk did have several unique qualifications (chaff, decoys, flares, leaflets and smoke) but these could hardly generate considerable activity, so overall the Skyhawk squadrons' Lebanon War experience was of a fairly low intensity. (via author)

sector as IDF troops advanced towards the town south of Beirut. H-Hour was 1400 hrs.

The Skyhawk's day as an IDF/AF SAM battery hunter were by now well and truly over, however. The Skyhawk was the lowest-level combat aircraft in then service, with its primary role being CAS. Yet since 1973 all Skyhawk pilots had trained to 'support and follow-up' Israeli SEAD operations. 'Support and follow-up' ensured that Skyhawks would participate at the beginning and the end of the operation that was at the time the most important and challenging mission ever flown by the IDF/AF.

'Support' covered dispensing massive amounts of chaff in order to blind enemy radars, dropping decoys aimed at luring enemy radar operators into activating their systems and then launching AGM-45 Shrike anti-radiation missiles against active radars. Obviously, the F-4Es with their precision-guided munitions were the IDF/AF's principal SAM battery destroyers, but the plan also included back-up attack aircraft armed with 'dumb' bombs that were to follow the Phantom IIs in regardless of whether they had succeeded in destroying the targeted SAMs. Skyhawks were not the main force of the follow-up wave, but several formations were assigned to this part of the mission.

Mole Cricket 19 was launched as planned, with intensive Skyhawk participation in the first suppression phase. The A-4s generated chaff clouds, released decoys and launched missiles. Suppression was achieved and the destruction wave was also successful. This meant that the back-up wave was redundant, and most of the planned Skyhawk formations did not take part in the closing phase. A few A-4s attacked, but all the others were diverted mid-air to CAS missions that included interdiction along roads in the Lebanon Valley – once at the heart of the engagement envelope of the supposedly mighty Syrian air defence force deployment.

None of the 14 Syrian surface-to-air batteries claimed destroyed by IDF/AF attack aircraft during *Mole Cricket 19* were credited to Skyhawk pilots, but their support of the suppression phase was crucial to the success of the following destruction wave. There can be little doubt that the annihilation of the Syrian air defence force deployment in the Lebanon Valley without a single IDF/AF casualty in return would have been impossible without the Skyhawks' blinding chaff and confusing decoys.

SKYHAWK SUNSET

Operation *Mole Cricket 19* changed the reality of air warfare. The superiority of the SAM over the aircraft was crushed. Air superiority was again the domain of air power, and an air-to-air battle. The fight for air superiority over the Lebanon Valley on 9 June 1982 ended a decade of air defence force superiority principally because the aircraft lacked the precision of the missile. Obviously, many factors influenced this trend, including communications, control, electronics and intelligence stand-off, but the precise surgical attack capability was the centrepiece of *Mole Cricket 19*.

Fighting continued past *Mole Cricket 19*. The air superiority battle was not a stand-alone clash, as the objective was to ensure air support for IDF forces advancing towards the Beirut-Damascus highway. Air superiority was achieved and air support was given, but the IDF had not set foot on the Beirut-Damascus highway by the time a ceasefire was imposed.

Day 5 Skyhawk activity intensified considerably because of the securing of air superiority and the proximity of IDF efforts to the Beirut-Damascus highway. Extensive CAS was flown in the Damur to Beirut sector, including aerial leaflet drops. Air strikes focused along the Beirut-Damascus highway and in the east along the Lebanon Valley. Operations in the latter sector included interdiction aimed at Syrian reinforcements.

From Day 1 to Day 4 of the Lebanon War, the Skyhawks' rules of engagement were shaped by the desire to achieve maximum survivability. The A-4s flew mostly CAS over lower risk sectors, and operated from medium altitude above the effective ceiling of most threats in these sectors. From Day 5 Skyhawk missions ranged deeper into the Lebanon Valley and along the Beirut-Damascus highway from Beirut in the west to the Syrian border in the east. Extended coverage of the Skyhawk force, and operations over higher risk sectors, were certainly facilitated by air superiority. It also allowed pilots to commence strafing runs on many missions from Day 5. Obviously, air superiority had been achieved against Syrian SAM batteries and fighters. *Mole Cricket 19* did not suppress or destroy the threats of AAA and shoulder-launched SAMs, yet A-4 pilots were confident enough to add strafing to their attack menu.

Skyhawks seldom flew at night during the June 1982 war, but the last night of the conflict (10/11 June) was an exception. Israeli intelligence identified a Syrian brigade on the move along the Lebanon Valley highway heading for the frontline. IDF/AF aircraft attacked the highway throughout the night and claimed destruction of the Syrian brigade.

Not yet equipped with night vision equipment, the Skyhawk pilots initially utilised illumination. Yet it was impossible to identify vehicles along the illuminated road. Later during that night, the A-4 pilots flew over the road without the aid of illumination. Instead, they looked for a faint white headlight or, better still, an occasional red braking light. When such lights were identified, the point in the road was bombed. Vehicles catching fire indicated success.

By the morning of Day 6, 12 June 1982, the three IDF main efforts were close to the Beirut-Damascus highway, the southern suburbs of Beirut in the west, the En Zhalta sector east of Beirut and pushing north along the Lebanese-Syrian border. The IDF/AF had total air superiority over the battlefield, but IDF forces failed to set foot on the Beirut-Damascus highway before the ceasefire at 1200 hrs. A little more than an hour before the ceasefire, a Flying Wing Squadron formation demonstrated the essence of air superiority. The formation departed Tel Nof at 1015 hrs for a CAS mission north of Lake Karoun, but en route to this sector, the formation's mission was changed to interdiction on the west side of the Lebanon Valley.

When a convoy of Syrian tanks was spotted, the leader ordered his pilots to release one bomb per run. Since the Skyhawks were armed with eight general purpose Mk 82 bombs each, they flew eight runs and then added four strafing passes. Only air superiority could enable such an amazing show of determination and force. The determined Skyhawk pilots could only claim five to six tanks, however, primarily because they did not attack with precision-guided munitions.

Although the ceasefire became effective at 1200 hrs, fighting continued. East of Beirut, the IDF 'crawled' north in a series of clashes to finally reach the Beirut-Damascus highway. It eventually linked up with the Lebanese Christian militia north of Beirut – a manoeuvre that placed the Lebanese capital under Israeli siege. Urban warfare followed until August 1982 when an agreement was reached and armed Palestinians evacuated Beirut from 21 August until 5 September.

Fighting did not end at this point either, with IDF/AF operations continuing until Israel completed its withdrawal from Lebanon in May 2000. That is why a full summary of Skyhawk operations in the Lebanon War can be difficult to report. Obviously, the 'official' Lebanon War timeframe lasted from 6 to 12 June 1982, but preparatory air strikes started on 4 June 1982, and post-war air operations continued in varying degrees of intensity for many months afterwards.

The Golden Eagle Squadron's Lebanon War timeframe was from 4 June until 12 August 1982, from the start of air strikes over Lebanon until the end of the bombing in the Beirut siege. During this period the Ramon-based Skyhawks flew 224 sorties, including 179 air support missions. These figures were typical for all five Skyhawk squadrons, and the spread of 1000 sorties over two months was clear evidence that the Lebanon War was an intensified interwar episode rather than a full-scale conflict like the Yom Kippur War.

Air strikes over Lebanon resumed in November 1983. The Palestinians were gone and the 'new' enemy was Iranian-sponsored and -trained Shia Islam organisations. The Flying Wing Squadron flew its first mission from Nevatim on 10 February 1984 when a section used LGBs to attack a house at Bhamdoun, east of Beirut along the highway to Damascus. Nine days later, the Flying Wing Squadron attacked another house at Bhamdoun, as did its sister unit the Flying Dragon Squadron, which was was still operating from Tel Nof. The latter attacked again on 2 June 1984 when two pairs of A-4s bombed a small island off Tripoli at sunset.

The Golden Eagle Squadron handed over the Skyhawk OTU course to the Flying Wing Squadron from the summer of 1985 as combat missions became more and more scarce. The sole significant mission flown during 1985 involved a Flying Wing Squadron raid on a headquarters at Chtaura, in the Lebanon Valley. The IDF/AF claimed the destruction of a HQ building and post-strike reports indicated that 40 men had been killed inside the dwelling.

A similar pattern followed in 1986, with one major Skyhawk air strike mission flown on 23 September when the Flying Tiger Squadron and the Flying Wing Squadron attacked two Palestinian targets. The Skyhawks were operating as part of an IDF/AF aerial campaign aimed at preventing the return of Palestinian organisations to Lebanon in the wake of the IDF withdrawal from most of the 1982 occupied territories to a 'security zone' north of the Israeli-Lebanese border in June 1985.

The two major phases of the Israeli withdrawal from Lebanon saw troops initially pulled back into the first security zone during 1985, followed by a total pullout from the country in 2000. However, this withdrawal did not prevent the continuation of low-intensity clashes escalating into major conflict. This pattern was repeated during the 1985-2000 timeframe, with two major clashes during 1993 and 1996, and ongoing smaller-scale operations in between.

The Skyhawk was by now nearing the end of a distinguished career. However, operations over Lebanon were now rather low-risk, so the IDF/AF rotated air strike assignment between all combat aircraft squadrons, and the Skyhawks flew as many missions as other, more advanced and more capable attack types. Israeli air strikes over Lebanon were sometimes sporadic, occasionally not flown for weeks or months, and from time to time concentrated into larger scale clashes. The Skyhawk squadrons, therefore, averaged an air strike or so per year, and a 'major' air campaign once every several years.

The A-4 squadrons' 1987 air strikes were flown in May, the Flying Dragon and the Flying Wing Squadrons attacking first on 1 May. Their targets were in the Sidon sector, and jets attacked with heavy 2,000-lb Mk 84 bombs. The Flying Tiger Squadron followed later in the month.

Operations intensified somewhat in 1988 when each squadron flew more than one air strike mission. The Nevatim squadrons started operations on 2 January 1988, with their objectives being Palestinian organisations in southern Lebanon. H-Hour was 2230 hrs, and the Skyhawks operated in three-ship formations. The jets made use of Israel Aircraft Industries Griffin LGBs for the first time in nighttime attack mission. The Flying Tiger Squadron attacked in March and the Nevatim Skyhawk units returned to Lebanon on 22 April. Two pairs, one from each squadron, attacked a PLO target north of Damur.

A Flying Wing Squadron four-ship formation bombed a target in southern Lebanon on 21 October, and all Skyhawk squadrons took part in Operations *Blue* and *Brown* – a combined IDF and IDF/AF assault on

The first operational mission from Nevatim air base was flown on 10 February 1984 when the Flying Wing Squadron attacked a target in Lebanon. The squadron moved from Tel Nof to Nevatim in October 1983 and was the Skyhawk force pioneer of laser-guided bomb delivery. A-4N tail number 338 was the lead ship in this attack and departed Nevatim with four laser-guided bombs and was photographed upon its return having expended only two bombs. This pair, which hit a house at Bhamdoun, was an interesting comparison with the usual Skyhawk attack pattern of four aircraft each lifting eight 500-lb Mk 82 bombs! (via author)

CHAPTER FIVE

Flying Tiger Squadron A-4N Skyhawk tail number 358 checked before taxiing out of its sun-shelter for an operational mission over Lebanon on 23 September 1986. The Skyhawk is loaded with four 360-kg bombs attached to a MER and was number 2 in a four-ship formation of similarly armed A-4Ns. Quite interestingly, the spare Skyhawk prepared for this mission was an A-4H. The tempo of 'routine security' missions was so low that each aircraft was prepared special-operation style with a spare aircraft and pilot, fully briefed and loaded for the task. The spare usually taxied along with the formation to the end of the runway apron where the aircraft attended the 'last chance' drill; sometimes, the spare even took off and flew with the formation until a pre-set point where it turned back to base. (via author)

Palestinian organization targets north of Damur during the night of 9/10 December. This operation was not wholly successful, but IDF/AF efforts secured a safe retreat of all troops involved. All Skyhawk squadrons flew conventional air support to cover the retreat except for the Flying Dragons, who were entrusted with a smoke screening mission.

A-4 strike intensity was maintained at a low level from 1989 to 1992. A high-intensity clash erupted in July 1993 when the IDF launched Operation *Coincidence 2*. From 25 to 31 July, air strikes hammered southern Lebanon with occasional deeper incursions. The effectiveness of precision-guided munitions was now beyond doubt, and within the A-4 force demand for the LGB-qualified Flying Wing Squadron was higher than demand for the Flying Tiger Squadron, which still lacked LGB capability. The Flying Wing flew 34 sorties during *Coincidence 2* while the Flying Tigers flew only 14.

An even higher-intensity clash was Operation *Grapes of Wrath* that Israel launched on 11 April 1996. Its objective was similar to *Coincidence 2* and *Peace for Galilee* – the elimination of the threat of attacks from Lebanese soil. *Grapes of Wrath* followed the pattern of previous operations, with massive Israeli artillery and air strikes against rocket launches from Lebanese territory. IDF/AF aircraft flew 2500 sorties from 11 to 27 April, and the Skyhawk sunset was more evident than ever. During the Yom Kippur War, the A-4 had flown nearly half the number of combat aircraft sorties generated. In *Grapes of Wrath* the Flying Tiger Squadron had accumulated just 70 sorties – less than half the number flown by units equipped with more modern combat aircraft.

RETIREMENT PLANS

The Skyhawk fleet did not undergo major technical modifications during the 1980s and 1990s. Minor changes included the fitment of a colour video recorder, modernised electrical systems and adaptation to the EHUD autonomous air combat manoeuvring instrumentation pod. The most significant operational change during this timeframe was the transition from free-fall bombs to precision LGBs.

The Flying Dragon Squadron joined the laser guided bomb trend after its sister squadron, the Flying Wing, pioneered this operational domain. A-4N tail number 401 was photographed at Nevatim on 3 March 1991 loaded with four 500-lb laser guided bombs prior to an operational mission over Lebanon. This was the fourth IDF/AF air strike across the Lebanese border during 1991 and was aimed at Palestinian vehicles north of Nabatiya in south Lebanon. (via author)

Flying Dragon Squadron A-4N Skyhawk tail number 401 on 'routine security' air-to-ground attack readiness at Nevatim in 1992. The Skyhawk is parked inside a sun-shelter for protection against the savage desert sun and armed with four 360-kg general purpose bombs attached to a MER under the fuselage, as well as two 500-lb laser guided bombs on the outer wing stations. The Skyhawk is ready for a call for either maximum-destruction 'carpet bombing' through unguided bombs or a surgical precision strike. (via author)

At the same time, the validity of strafing in the modern battlefield was questioned. Doubts began to sink in during 1990, and the first step was the omission of low-level strafing training from the OTU syllabus. Nine years later the A-4's cannon-strafing qualification was discontinued.

The three most prominent features of Israeli Skyhawk upgrades were 'barrel', cannon and Crystal. The cannon qualification was gone and the 'barrel' nozzle extension now played a less significant role following the introduction of flares as a defensive countermeasure against heat-seeking missiles. The third element, Crystal, was beginning to show its age, but initial IDF/AF long term planning in the 1990s did not include any kind of Skyhawk upgrade. Indeed, the official view throughout the 1990s was that the A-4 would be retired in 2005. By 2002 it became obvious that the Skyhawk would remain in service well past 2005. The IDF/AF had not purchased a new advanced trainer to replace the TA-4, as it was felt that the aircraft still provided valuable training for F-16 OTU course graduates. Training issues rather than operational considerations were at the heart of the Skyhawk service extension plans.

From the 1980s the electronic gap between the Skyhawk and IDF/AF's advanced combat aircraft grew wider and wider. If the Skyhawk retirement date was 2005, then the old Crystal system could soldier on, but service-life revision triggered an urgent requirement for one more Skyhawk upgrade.

Initially, the Skyhawk upgrade was limited to training capabilities. This involved installation of a RADA Electronic Industries Autonomous Combat Evaluation (ACE) internal autonomous air combat manoeuvring instrumentation system to replace the stopgap EHUD pod. The RADA ACE-II was installed in the Skyhawk fleet from 2002.

Satisfaction with the ACE-II kick-started a broader avionics upgrade project, with RADA as prime contractor. A validation phase contract was awarded in January 2003 and a full-scale upgrade contract followed in January 2004. The upgrade focuses on the ACE-II system, effectively replacing Crystal. At the heart of the upgrade are two 'black boxes', the Mission and Fire-Control Unit (MFU) and the Ring Laser Gyro Navigation System (RNS). The IDF/AF preferred RNS as a cheaper alternative to Embedded GPS INS, and essentially RNS feeds six-axis positional data of the aircraft in space to the MFU that controls the mission through navigation and weapons delivery.

Cockpit displays have been modernised with the insertion of a multi-function display. The old A-4N head-up display has been retained, but

CHAPTER FIVE

The Flying Wing Squadron used two families of laser guided bombs during the 1990s: the US-manufactured kits and the indigenous Israel Aircraft Industries Griffin. A-4N Skyhawk tail number 309 was photographed in the early morning hours of 22 February 1996 prior to a strike mission over Lebanon. The Skyhawk was armed with 500-lb Griffin laser guided bombs and flew lead to a Mk 82-loaded Skyhawk. The pair attacked a Hizballah target at Jabel Safi, Lebanon. This was the third IDF/AF air strike over Lebanon in 1996. (via author)

the presentation was improved through inputs from a team of Skyhawk and Fighting Falcon pilots. ACE-II generated data files are synchronised with the output of a head-up display camera. The synchronised data allows a replay of the complete mission in a ground debrief station. RADA offered to add virtual radar capability too, but the IDF/AF rejected this offer on cost grounds. Virtual radar remains an option that can be easily added through RADA software updates and installation of a Rafael data link.

The RADA A-4 upgrade project covered the A-4N and TA-4 fleet of the Flying Tiger Squadron. As the IDF/AF's largest combat aircraft squadron, the Flying Tigers' three tasks are supplying flying hours to the Flying School Advanced Training Squadron (since 1994), conducting the OTU course (from 2003) and maintaining its status as an operational squadron. Almost half of the Flying Tiger Squadron's inventory of Skyhawks consists of two-seat TA-4 models that originally lacked head-up displays and inertial navigation systems. The RADA upgrade also covered a common avionics standard among the Flying Tigers' TA-4 and A-4N models.

The Improved Skyhawk prototype first flew in December 2004. The upgrade was competed by the end of 2005, with the objective being to extend Skyhawk service until 2020, both as a combat aircraft and as a trainer. To complement the upgrade, the IDF/AF contracted Skyhawk maintenance to Israel Aircraft Industries. The ten-year maintenance contract was announced in December 2004 and covered A-Level (squadron), B-Level (base) and D-Level (depot) maintenance under a 'power by the hour' scheme – payment by output (flying hours), rather

The IDF/AF fighter community's OTU course was transferred from the Golden Eagle Squadron to the Flying Wing Squadron in 1985. The Flying Wing Squadron initially used Air Combat Maneuvering Instrumentation pods to enhance training. During the 1990s, the IDF/AF introduced an internal RADA Autonomous Air Combat Maneuvering Instrumentation system to the F-16 fleet and considered fitting the Skyhawk fleet with similar equipment. However, at the time the Skyhawk was scheduled for retirement by 2005, so BVR Systems announced in November 1999 its lease of EHUD Autonomous Air Combat Maneuvering Instrumentation pods to the IDF/AF. These were used to enhance the training standards of the Flying Wing Squadron OTU course. A-4N Skyhawk tail number 421 was photographed at Nevatim in 2002 with EHUD pod under the right-hand outer wing station. (via author)

In late 2002 the Skyhawk celebrated 35 years in Israeli service, a remarkable achievement for a warplane that first flew back in 1954. Yet although signs of age had appeared, IDF/AF planners realized that the Skyhawk would not retire by 2005 and plans were forwarded to rejuvenate the old warrior for 10-15 years of service-life extension. (via author)

than inputs (materials and hours). The old Skyhawk made history again as the first Israeli combat aircraft maintained by a commercial contractor.

Skyhawk operations over Lebanon ended in the wake of Israel's retreat from the country in May 2000. From September 2000 the focus of IDF/AF 'routine security' operations shifted to the Palestinian Authority, with noctunal illumination becoming a Skyhawk 'specialist' mission. Yet the pattern of an occasional flare up in Lebanon did not disappear, and the second Lebanon War erupted in July 2006. Almost 40 years after entering IDF/AF service, the Skyhawk was not expected to be at the heart of the battle. While Israeli combat aircraft flew nearly 10,000 sorties from 12 July to 14 August 2006, the A-4s flew 240 sorties that covered electronic support, illumination and leaflet drops.

The Skyhawk is certainly no longer one of the foremost or important IDF/AF aircraft, but it is still a valuable asset – a stubborn little attack aircraft that has always been there when needed. Ageing as it is, the RADA Improved Skyhawk upgrade and the ten-year 'power by the hour' contract indicate that the IDF/AF plans to retain the Skyhawk in service until 2015 at the very least. There is hope therefore that sometime in late 2017 or early 2018 an appropriately austere ceremony will celebrate the Skyhawk's Golden Jubilee in Israeli service!

Flying Tiger Squadron TA-4 Skyhawks prepare to take off from Hatzerim on a routine training mission in the late summer of 2006, shortly after the end of the second Lebanon War. By then, all of the Flying Tiger Squadron A-4Ns and TA-4s were upgraded to common RADA Improved Skyhawk standard. Roughly half of the Flying Tiger Squadron's inventory of Skyhawks are TA-4s, all of which are fully operational and function as electronic-warfare platforms in addition to their day-to-day duties such as training Flying School undergraduate students (Fighter Advanced Training Squadron and Fighter Navigators Training Squadron air cadets) and OTU course postgraduate students. (via author)

APPENDICES

DATE	THEATRE	SQUADRON	TYPE	TAIL NUMBER	PILOT	FATE
19 August 1969	Egypt	102	A-4H	02	Ashkenazi	Prisoner of War
9 September 1969	Egypt	109	A-4H	26	Ronen	Missing in Action
16 January 1970	Egypt	102	A-4H	76	Peleg	Killed in Action
6 October 1973	Syria	109	A-4H	87	Eitan	Killed in Action
6 October 1973	Syria	110	A-4E	235	Yardeni	Retrieved
6 October 1973	Egypt	102	A-4H	54	Katziri	Prisoner of War
6 October 1973	Egypt	102	A-4H	24	Karp	Retrieved
6 October 1973	Egypt	102	A-4H	64	Sadan	Killed in Action
7 October 1973	Syria	102	A-4H	53	Horowitz	Killed in Action
7 October 1973	Syria	110	A-4E	255	Lev	Killed in Action
7 October 1973	Egypt	115	A-4N	312	Ash	Missing in Action
7 October 1973	Egypt	102	A-4H	68	Daller	Killed in Action
7 October 1973	Syria	116	A-4E	211	Shamir	Retrieved
7 October 1973	Egypt	102	A-4H	60	Avital	Killed in Action
7 October 1973	Egypt	109	A-4H	34	Lapidot	Killed in Action
7 October 1973	Egypt	110	A-4E	267	Ostraicher	Killed in Action
7 October 1973	Egypt	110	A-4E	239	Bar-Ziv	Killed in Action
7 October 1973	Syria	115	A-4N	361	Rosenblum	Killed in Action
8 October 1973	Syria	110	A-4E	226	Lobashevsky	Retrieved
8 October 1973	Egypt	115	A-4N	366	Rozen	Prisoner of War
8 October 1973	Egypt	115	A-4N	363	Bashan	Killed in Action
8 October 1973	Egypt	102	A-4H	04	Schwager	Retrieved
8 October 1973	Egypt	102	TA-4	46	Ben-Eliezer	Killed in Action
9 October 1973	Egypt	116	A-4E	221	Litani	Killed in Action
9 October 1973	Egypt	102	A-4H	66	Reinberg	Prisoner of War
9 October 1973	Egypt	102	A-4H	50	Gardi	Prisoner of War
9 October 1973	Egypt	116	A-4E	229	Shelach	Killed in Action
9 October 1973	Egypt	102	A-4H	90	Kadmon	Retrieved
9 October 1973	Syria	110	A-4E	245	Sharon	Retrieved
9 October 1973	Egypt	110	A-4E	218	Lev	Missing in Action
9 October 1973	Syria	109	A-4H	?	?	Retrieved
9 October 1973	Egypt	115	A-4N	398	Shaked	Killed in Action
9 October 1973	Egypt	116	A-4E	204	Matos	Prisoner of War
9 October 1973	Syria	109	A-4H	10	Kedmi	Retrieved
10 October 1973	Syria	109	A-4H	65	Ben-Ari	Killed in Action
11 October 1973	Syria	102	A-4H	83	Guy	Prisoner of War
11 October 1973	Syria	102	A-4H	08	Tron	Prisoner of War
11 October 1973	Syria	102	A-4H	58	Nesher	Prisoner of War
11 October 1973	Syria	115	A-4N	378	Schneider	Prisoner of War
11 October 1973	Syria	115	A-4N	322	Ofer	Killed in Action
11 October 1973	Syria	116	A-4E	241	Hertz	Prisoner of War
12 October 1973	Syria	109	A-4H	27	Baster	Killed in Action
12 October 1973	Syria	110	A-4E	257	Peleg	Retrieved
13 October 1973	Syria	109	TA-4	67	Gerzon	Prisoner of War
13 October 1973	Syria	109	A-4H	01	Arad	Retrieved
13 October 1973	Egypt	102	TA-4	43	Ofri	Killed in Action
15 October 1973	Syria	109	A-4H	?	Raviv	Retrieved
15 October 1973	Syria	109	A-4H	52	Saar	Killed in Action
16 October 1973	Egypt	102	A-4H	51	Eyal	Killed in Action
17 October 1973	Egypt	110	A-4E	222	Poraz	Killed in Action
17 October 1973	Egypt	102	A-4H	59	Shoham	Retrieved
18 October 1973	Egypt	109	A-4H	03	Sharon	Retrieved
18 October 1973	Egypt	109	A-4H	99	Fonk	Killed in Action
18 October 1973	Egypt	110	A-4E	253	Sharon	Prisoner of War
18 October 1973	Egypt	110	A-4E	?	?	Retrieved
21 October 1973	Syria	109	A-4H	69	Lahav	Killed in Action
19 April 1974	Syria	North Knights	A-4E	70	Dobnov	Killed in Action
6 June 1982	Lebanon	Flying Dragon	A-4N	334	Achiaz	Prisoner of War

ACTIVATION YEAR	BASE	SQUADRON	DETAILS
1967	Ramat David	109	A-4H
1967	Hatzor	102	A-4H, to Hatzerim in 1968, A-4E from 1973, A-4N from 1986
1969	Tel Nof	115	A-4H, A-4N from 1973, to Nevatim in 1984
1971	Tel Nof	116	A-4E, A-4N from 1973, to Nevatim in 1983
1971	Ramat David	110	A-4E, A-4H from 1977
1972	Hatzerim	Flying School Fighter Advance Training	TA-4 and A-4H with A-4N from 1990
1973	Etszion	Golden Eagle	A-4E, A-4N from 1976, to Ramon in 1981
1976	Etszion	Shattering Parrot	A-4E and A-4N
1978	Hatzerim	Flying Ibex	A-4E, A-4F, A-4H and A-4N

NOTE 1   All squadrons flew TA-4 Skyhawks
NOTE 2   From 1973 onwards many squadrons flew mixed fleets

COLOUR PLATES

1
A-4H BuNo 155242, Palmdale, California, 1967
Israel's first 48 A-4H Skyhawks were assigned US Navy Bureau Numbers 155242 to 155289 and delivered to Israel as Operation *Rugby* aircraft from December 1967. The first was US Navy Bureau Number 155242, which first flew on 27 October 1967 but was not among the first four Skyhawks shipped to Israel in December 1967. All Skyhawks manufactured for Israel were painted in the IAF post-Six Day War standard camouflage scheme.

2
A-4H IAF tail number 01, No 109 Sqn, Ramat David, 1968
Upon arrival in Israel, the first Israeli Skyhawk, A-4H US Navy Bureau Number 155242, was assigned IAF number 5301 with 'tail number' 01 painted on both sides of the nose section. Issued to 109 Squadron at Ramat David, Skyhawk 01 served that unit until lost in combat during the October 1973 Yom Kippur War.

3
A-4H IAF tail number 69, No 115 Sqn, Tel Nof, 1969
The follow-up *Rugby* contract enabled the IAF to activate a third A-4H unit, 115 Squadron based at Tel Nof. The selection process of the 102 Squadron and 115 Squadron motifs have become an IAF legend. The 102 Squadron set-up team initially presented a dragon for approval as the squadron badge, but this was rejected. The somewhat offended set-up team decided to present for approval a theme that they thought would certainly be rejected, so that the dragon would be approved as the default option. The selected figure was a smiling tiger copied from a figure in the comics, but to the amazement of the 102 Squadron set-up team the tiger was approved! Then, to their dismay, the dragon was approved as the 115 Squadron badge.

4
A-4E IAF tail number 208, No 116 Sqn, Tel Nof, 1971
Rugby D A-4E 208 was unloaded at Ashdod port on 18 February 1971, issued to 116 Squadron at Tel Nof, survived the Yom Kippur War and became Skyhawk 808.

5
A-4H IAF tail number 738, No 102 Sqn, Hatzerim, 1971
102 Squadron initially used two-digit 'tail numbers' (actually painted on the nose of the aircraft) but progressively introduced the prefix 7. After the Yom Kippur War a standard numbering system was introduced and Skyhawk 738 became A-4H 238.

6
A-4E IAF tail number 253, No 110 Sqn, Ramat David, 1972
US Navy Bureau Number 152032 became IAF number 5253 and served 110 Squadron as Skyhawk 253 while 102 Squadron operated A-4H IAF number 5353 as Skyhawk 753; both were lost during the Yom Kippur War.

7
A-4N US Navy BuNu 158726, Palmdale, California, 1972
The second Skyhawk model developed specifically to suit Israel requirements was the A-4N Skyhawk II that first flew in June 1972. US Navy Bureau Number 158726 was the first of 117 A-4Ns, including seven Yom Kippur War attrition replacements.

8
TA-4H IAF tail number 743, Flying School Advanced Training Squadron, Hatzerim, 1972
Skyhawk 43 was initially a 115 Squadron aircraft, then issued to 116 Squadron, then assigned to 102

Squadron and then handed over to the Flying School Fighter Advanced Training Squadron in October 1972.

9
A-4N IAF tail number 322, No 115 Sqn, Tel Nof, 1973
US Navy Bureau Number 158726 became IAF number 2322 or Skyhawk tail number 322 and would have become Skyhawk 422 if not lost during the Yom Kippur War.

10
A-4H IAF tail number 278, Valley Squadron, Ramat David, 1975
Initially flying as Skyhawk 778 in the pre-October 1973 era, this Skyhawk was issued to the Valley Squadron after the Yom Kippur War but lost in an accident while in Flying Ibex Squadron service during 1981.

11
A-4E IAF tail number 889, Knights of the North Squadron, Ramat David, 1975
The Knights of the North Squadron flew the A-4E until 1977 when the A-4H was introduced. At the time the cannon replacement programme was still running, but 889 was still armed with 20 mm cannon. Not all of the A-4E Skyhawks were eventually modified.

12
A-4E IAF tail number 866, Shattering Parrot Squadron, Etszion, 1976
Three single-seat Skyhawks with tail number 66 flew during the Yom Kippur War, but only A-4E Skyhawk 266 survived to become Skyhawk 866, as indicated by both the prefix numbering and the IAF-style air-intake warning.

13
A-4H IAF tail number 272, Flying Tiger Squadron, Hatzerim, 1977
The torpedo-boat killer started its IAF career in 115 Squadron service during the War of Attrition and was a 102 Squadron aircraft (as Skyhawk 772) during the Yom Kippur War.

14
A-4N IAF tail number 413, Golden Eagle Squadron, Ramon, 1981
The US AGM-prefixed weapons in IAF Skyhawk service were the AGM-12 Bullpup air-to-surface missile, the AGM-45 Shrike anti-radiation missile and the AGM-62 Walleye guided glide bomb. The Skyhawks used all three during the Yom Kippur War but only the Shrike during the Lebanon War in 1982.

15
A-4N IAF tail number 344, Flying Dragon Squadron, Nevatim, 1984
More than 100 A-4N Skyhawks entered IAF service, so some had identical 'last two' tail number digits. One of these pairs was Skyhawk 344 that served the Flying Dragon Squadron and Skyhawk 444 in the Golden Eagle Squadron.

16
A-4F IAF tail number 604, Flying Ibex Squadron, Hatzerim, 1986
The fourth Skyhawk squadron to introduce characteristic rudder paintwork was the Flying Ibex Squadron, which adopted a simple yellow rudder scheme.

17
A-4N IAF tail number 407, Flying Tiger Squadron, Hatzerim, 1986
Another A-4N 'last two' pair was Flying Dragon Squadron Skyhawk 307 and Flying Tiger Squadron Skyhawk 407. The latter unit operated Skyhawks with a mix of blue rudder and blue rudder with white stripes during the 1980s.

18
A-4N IAF tail number 401, Flying Dragon Squadron, Nevatim, 1988
In similar fashion, in the 1980s, the Flying Dragon Squadron had Skyhawks with 'negative' and 'positive' rudder artwork designs, of red rudder with white stripes and white rudder with red stripes.

19
TA-4J IAF tail number 705, Flying School Advanced Training Squadron, Hatzerim, 1988
Skyhawk trainers had their rudders and nose sections painted orange during the 1980s when the Flying School Fighter Advanced Training Squadron flew both single- and two-seat Skyhawks.

20
A-4N IAF tail number 328, Flying School Advanced Training Squadron/Flying Tiger Squadron, Hatzerim, 1992
The Flying School Fighter Advanced Training Squadron and the Flying Tiger Squadron were combined in 1990. The orange rudder and nose paintwork was applied to all aircraft while the Flying Tiger Squadron badge was painted on the left-hand side of the vertical stabilizer and the Flying School Fighter Advanced Training Squadron badge was painted on the right-hand side.

21
A-4N IAF tail number 302, Flying Tiger Squadron, Hatzerim, 1996
The Flying Tiger Squadron was restored in 1994 as a frontline unit supplying training services to the Flying School but the identifying blue rudder with white stripes did not make a comeback. Larger-than-usual IAF badges were standard practice with the IAF in 1990s exercises with foreign air forces.

22
A-4N IAF tail number 310, Flying Tiger Squadron, Hatzerim, 2001
Instead of the old blue rudder with white stripes, from 1997 the Flying Tiger Squadron introduced a

larger vertical stabilizer artwork of a definitely not smiling winged tiger.

23
A-4N IAF tail number 342, Flying Tiger Squadron, Hatzerim, 2003

The first RADA Improved Skyhawk was A-4N tail number 342, US Navy Bureau Number 159808. More than 30 years had elapsed since Crystal was designed and the new system was significantly smaller and lighter. Technically, the 'hump' avionics bay could have been removed from the backs of Improved Skyhawks but to avoid complicated weight and balance issues, the IAF and RADA decided to retain the old, useless Crystal components 'as is'.

24
TA-4 IAF tail number 725, Flying Tiger Squadron, Hatzerim, 2007

The only significant external evidence of the RADA Improved Skyhawk is the Hebrew titles painted on both sides of the fuselage. The Improved Skyhawk project achieved common capabilities, since prior to the RADA upgrade the A-4N was Crystal-equipped and the TA-4 was not. The Skyhawk cannon qualification had been discarded a decade previously, but not all of the TA-4 Skyhawks had had their cannon removed and the wing leading-edge smoothed as Skyhawk 725 has.

ACKNOWLEDGEMENTS

The author would like to offer his gratitude to A-4 Skyhawk aircrews and maintainers and friends and colleagues who contributed to the production of this volume. Special thanks to Israeli master modeller Asher Roth, to Yehuda Borovik of BIAF Israel Air and Space Magazine, to Dr Ran Yahalom and to the Israeli Censorship Board who reviewed and approved this title for publication. To save space, as well as to avoid confusion and repetition, no ranks are mentioned in the text. Identification of Israeli A-4 units in the post-Yom Kippur War era by names, rather than by numbers as is the military custom, is a requirement of the Israeli Censorship Board.

INDEX

References to illustrations are shown in **bold**.

Achiaz, Aharon 82
Agassi, Yaakov 14, 28
Agmon, Yoram **34**
Artzi, Aki 10
Ash, Shimon 42
Ashkenazi, Nissim **11**, 11*bis*, 13, 15*bis*, 21
Avital, Shai **41**

Bar-Lev, Haim **15**
Barrel tailpipe modification **51**, 60, **62**, 73, 74, 78, **80**, 89
Bashan, Zvika 46
Baster, Irik 24, **50**, 50
Ben-Ari, Yehuda 49
Ben-Barak, Zur 10
Ben-Dov, Giora **front cover**(4), 25–6
Ben-Nun, Assaf **18**, 27–8
Ben-Rom, Shmulik 47
Bina, Uri 38
buddy refuelling 17, 24

chaff dropping 59, 73, 84
combat statistics 72–3

Dagan, Arieh 13–14, 14, 19–20, **20**, 42
Daller, Libi 42
Dassault Mirage III 6, 16, 19, 25, 74
Dassault Mystere **6**, 13, **14**, 30, 72, 73
Dassault Ouragan **6**, 6, 31, 72, 73
Dassault Super Mystere **6**, 6*bis*, **51**, 59–60
Deversoir bridgehead 53, 55, 56, 58
Dobnov, Aryeh 74
Dotan, David 46
Dotan, Ezra 'Baban' **front cover**(4), 25–6, **26**
Douglas A-4E Skyhawks 29–30, **34**, 40, **47**; 30mm DEFA cannon 31, 89; Tail No 208 pl**65**(93); Tail No 211 **30**, 43; Tail No 216 **45**; Tail No 226 **46**; Tail No 235 **39**; Tail No 236 **31**; Tail No 245 **49**, **59**; Tail No 253 59, pl**66**(93); Tail No 257 **52**; Tail No 835 **39**; Tail No 862 **74**; Tail No 866 pl**67**(94); Tail No 889 pl**67**(94); Tail No 899 **81**; US Navy BuNo 150034 **63**
Douglas A-4F Crystal Skyhawks, Tail No 612 **77**; Douglas A-4F Skyhawks 8; Tail No 604 pl**68**(94)
Douglas A-4H Crystal Skyhawks 30–1, 32, 33, 33–4, 42, 89; Tail No 11 **64**; Tail No 25 **64**; Tail No 32 **34**
Douglas A-4H Skyhawks 9, **13**, 13, **19**; 30mm DEFA cannon 26–7, **27**, 28, 89; endurance 16–17; bomb load 15, **16**, 29; Snakeye retarded bombs 19, **21**, 21, 22; BuNo 155242 (Tail No 01) **53**, pl**65**(93); BuNo 155244 (Tail No 03) **14**, **17**; BuNo 155245 **15**; BuNo 155246 **15**; Tail No 01 (BuNo 155242) **53**, pl**65**(93); Tail No 03 (BuNo 155244) **14**, **17**, **26**; Tail No 04 **47**; Tail No 08 **51**; Tail No 17 **17**; Tail No 22 **57**; Tail No 23 **64**, **91**; Tail No 24 **29**; Tail No 26 **20**; Tail No 27 **18**, **50**; Tail No 34 **27**; Tail No 36 **42**; Tail No 50 **22**, **50**; Tail No 51 **55**; Tail No 55 **57**; Tail No 60 **41**; Tail No 61 **17**; Tail No 62 **21***bis*; Tail No 67 **56**; Tail No 69 pl**65**(93); Tail No 87 **35**; Tail No 90 **51**; Tail No 92 **24**; Tail No 99 **58**; Tail No 130 **17**; Tail No 229 **72**, **77**; Tail No 235 **77**; Tail No 241 **79**; Tail No 272 pl**68**(94); Tail No 278 pl**67**(94); Tail No 520 **54**; Tail No 738 pl**66**(93)
Douglas A-4N Skyhawks 30–1, 31, 33, 34, 42; Tail No 302 pl**70**(94); Tail No 306 **77**; Tail No 308 **76**; Tail No 309 **90**; Tail No 310 pl**70**(94-5); Tail No 322 (US Navy BuNo 158726) **33**, pl**67**(94); Tail No 327 **80**; Tail No 328 pl**69**(94); Tail No 332 **80**; Tail No 338 **87**; Tail No 342 pl**70**(95); Tail No 343 **77**; Tail No 344 pl**68**(94); Tail No 354 **75**; Tail No 356 **80**; Tail No 358 **88**; Tail No 376 **62**, **80**; Tail No 377 **78**; Tail No 392 **77**, **80**; Tail No 393 **84**; Tail No 401 pl**69**(94), **88**, **89**;

Tail No 405 **82**; Tail No 407 pl**69**(94); Tail No 413 pl**68**(94); Tail No 421 **2–3**, **90**; US Navy BuNo 158726 pl**66**(93)
Douglas TA-4F Skyhawks, Tail No 164 **76**
Douglas TA-4H Skyhawks: bomb load **23**, 49; electronic warfare platforms **91**; night intruders 23; observation missions 50, 52; Tail No 45 **32**; Tail No 66 **48**; Tail No 725 pl**70**(95); Tail No 743 **23**, **53**, pl**66**(93–4)
Douglas TA-4J Skyhawks, Tail No 705 pl**69**(94)

EHUD Autonomous Air Combat Manoevering pods 88, 89, **90**
Eitan, Hanan **35**, 36
Eshkol, Prime Minister Levy **15**
Eyal, Menachem **55**, 55
Ezuz, Arik 11

Flying School Advanced Training Squadron 31, **32**, 35
Fonk, Gershon 57, **58**
Franklin D Roosevelt, USS (aircraft carrier) 62
Furman, Giora 15

Gadish, Ami 34, 37
General Dynamics F-16 Fighting Falcon 74, **77**, 77
Gloster Meteor **6**, 6
Golan Heights 37, 39, 41, 43–4, 45, 48, 49, 50, 51, 52, 58
Golan, Itzhak 43–4, 45, 47–8
Goren, Ran 24, **32**

Harel, Norik **25**
Harlev, Rafi 11
Hatzerim air base **19**, 20, **47**, **56**, **91**
Hatzor air base 9–10, 10, 15, 16
Hillel, Arie 10
Hod, Moti **13**, 13–14, **19**, **47**

Israel Aircraft Industries Kfir 74, 75, 77

Karp, Mati 39–40
Kashtan, Menachem 24
Katziri, Yishay 39
Kochva, Yachin 37, 38
Koren, A Yehuda 16, **18**

Lahav, Eitan 61
Lebanon 74, 75–6, 78, 79, 82–4, 85–8, 91
Lev, Rafi 42
Lev, Zorik 47
Litani, Yaniv **45**

McDonnell Douglas F-4E Phantom II 6, 12, 23, 29, 32, 40, 42, 47, 52, 53, 55, 57, 59, 61, 84
Melnik, Moshe **21**, 22
MiG-17s **front cover**(4), 25, 51
MiG-21s 7, 28, 42*bis*, 49, 53, 56
missiles: AGM-12 Bullpup air-to-ground; AGM-45 Shrike anti-radiation 9, 29, 30, 32, 52, 84; AGM-62 Walleye TV guided 29, 30, 49, 52, 54, 58, 76; AIM-9B Sidewinder air-to-air 9, 30; LGB (Laser Guided Bomb) 77, 86, 87, **88**, 88, **90**; napalm delivery 19, **20**, 21
Mount Hermon 58, 61, 62, 64, 73

Nevatim air base **87**, 89

Ofri, Ran 52
Operation *Battery* **18**
Operation *Blossom* 23–4
Operation *Boxer* 18–20
Operation *Challenge 4* 40–3
Operation *Cracker 22* 56–7, 58
Operation *Goring Syria* 36
Operation *Litani* 75–6
Operation *Model 5* 43–4

Operation *Mole Cricket 19* 82–3, 84–5
Operation *Rugby* 8, 9
Peled, Beni 15, 34, 37, 43, **47**
Peleg, Dov 24
PLO targets 16, 24–6, 32–3, 75–6, 78, 79, 80–1, 87–8
Poraz, Maoz 56
Prigat, Eliezer **17**

RADA A-4 upgrade project 89–90, **90**
Ramat David air base 9–10, 10, 13, 30, 45*bis*, 46, **75**
Ramon air base 77, 79, **82**
Rom, Giora 34, 37–8
 Tulip 4 37
Ronen, Hagai **11**, 11, 13, 15, **20**, 22
Ronen, Ran 34, 37, 47
Rozen, Zvi 45

Saar, Gabi **54**, 54
Sadan, Ehud 40
Sarig, Yossi **8**, 10, **11**, 12–13, 13, **15**, 15*bis*, 19
Schelach, Udi 47, 48
Schneider, Michey 37
SEAD (suppression of air defences) 19–20, 21, 22, 27, 29, 32, 55, 84
Shadmi, Ohad 10, **11**, 11, 13, **14**, 15*bis*, **18**, 27
Shaked, Mario 47–8
Sharon, Gideon 57
Shelach, Udi **17**, 24
Six Day War 11, 13, 72–3
SNCASO Vautour II **6**, 6, 30
Snir, Asher 25
Squadrons:
 Flying Dragon 78, 80, 81, 81–2, 83, 86, 87
 Flying Ibex 75, 76, **78**
 Flying Tiger pl**71**, 73, 87*bis*, 88, 90, **91**
 Flying Wing 72, 74, **75**, 75, 76, **77**, 77, 78*bis*, 79, **80**, 86*bis*, 87, **90**
 Golden Eagle **34**, 34, 35, **52**, pl**71**, 72, 74, 75, **76**, 79*bis*, **81**, 81, 86
 Knights of the North **74**, 74, 77
 No. 102 **15**, 15–16, 16, **19**, 21, 23–4, **24**, 28, **29**, 35, 39–40, 42, **48**, **55**, 55, 56, **64**, pl**71**, 72
 No. 109 10, **14**, 15, 16, **18**, 18, 24, 27, 33, **34**, 35, 42, 43, 45–6, 49*bis*, 50, 51, **54**, 54, 57, **60**, 61, 62, 64, pl**71**, 72
 No. 110 30, **31**, 35, **39**, 39, 42–3, 43, 45, **49**, 49, 50, 56, 57, pl**71**, 72
 No. 115 **17**, 17, **21**, 21–2, 24, 31, 32, **33**, 34, 35, 37–8, 42*bis*, 43–4, 45, 49, 50, 51–2, 62, pl**71**, 72
 No. 116 **30**, 30, 34, 35, 40, 43*bis*, 45, 49, 50, 51, 56, 57, 58–9, pl**71**, 72
 Shattering Parrot 74, 77
 Valley **73**, 74, 75
Suez Canal 17, 18–20, 23, 24, 27, 28, 32, 39–40, 41–2, 45, 46, 53, 60, 63
Suez City 64, 73

Tel Nof air base 13, 17, **30**, 30, 37, 45, 47, 62, **77**

UN Security Council Resolution 338 62
US emergency aid Skyhawks 61–2, **63***bis*, pl**66**(93), 73

War of Attrition 17, 18, 20–4, 27–9, 81
Weizman, Ezer, IDF/AF Commander **8**, 8, 10

Yakir, Avraham 37, 38
Yardeni, Yanki **39**, 39
Yarom, Uri **9**
Yoeli, Aharon **9**, 11
Yom Kippur War 35–64, 72–3
Yosef, Rami 37

Zohar, Beni **46**